Hell Upon Earth

and

Satan's Harvest Home

Hell Upon Earth

and

Satan's Harvest Home

Edited with an Introduction by
Haley Ruffner

Whitlock Publishing
Alfred, NY

Hell Upon Earth first published in 1729.

Satan's Harvest Home first published in 1749.

First Whitlock Publishing edition 2016

Whitlock Publishing
P.O. Box 472
Alfred, NY 14802

ISBN 978-1-943115-15-0

This book was set in Adobe Garamond Pro on acid-free paper that meets ANSI standards for archival quality.

TABLE OF CONTENTS

Acknowledgements

Thank you to Dr. Grove for offering infinite help, unending patience, and guidance every step of the way.

Note on the Text

For both works, I have preserved archaic eighteenth-century spellings. I have also kept the extensive capitalization of nouns found in the first-edition texts.

INTRODUCTION

Published anonymously in 1729, *Hell Upon Earth: Or the Town in an Uproar. Occasion'd by the late horrible Scenes of Forgery, Perjury, Street-Robbery, Murder, Sodomy, and other shocking Impieties* is an early example of a conduct book. It was sold in London for the price of one shilling. The beginning of the work details the impieties that take place by the hour in an average day, followed by a more thorough look into the nuances of various sins, their origins, and their effects on society.

Satan's Harvest Home, fully titled *Satan's Harvest Home: or the Present State of Whorecraft, Adultery, Fornication, Procuring, Pimping, Sodomy, and the Game of Flatts, (Illustrated by an Authentick and Entertaining Story), And other Satanic Works, daily propagated in this good Protestant Kingdom* was published anonymously in 1749. It appeared as a pamphlet in London and covered, as is evident from its lengthy title, various aspects of sexual misconduct purportedly rampant in England. The section regarding the "Game of Flatts" was one of the first historical references to lesbianism in England. The entirety of *Satan's Harvest Home* is mostly plagiarized from a 1734 work called *Pretty Doings in a Protestant Nation* by Father Poissin, originally written in French. "The Petit Maitre," a poem condemning men who dress like women, appears at the end of the work.

Conduct Books

Conduct books such as *Satan's Harvest Home* and *Hell Upon Earth* are a staple of early modern literature in Europe; they emphasize the individual's ability to learn manners and lay out in clear terms the social norms that are expected to maintain one's virtue.[1] Although conduct books grew increasingly popular during the eighteenth century, the first known one was penned on papyrus by Egyptian king Ptah-Hotep in 2200 B.C.E. It was essentially a letter from the leader to his son that listed a series of virtues by which to live and has served as a model for later works.[2] *Hell Upon Earth* and *Satan's Harvest Home* function more as critiques of poor behavior rather than instructions for virtuous living, but they function well within the context of conduct books due to their popularity in the mid-1700s.

The ambiguous meaning of "virtue" is a central issue of conduct books and explains the wide range of content found in the genre; virtue varies depending on age, gender, personal beliefs, and social status, and thus it cannot be labeled in one definitive classification. While it can be vaguely defined as "moral goodness," even that did not apply to everyone; a woman seeking employment outside of the home was generally assumed to be a whore, whereas it was socially acceptable for men to work.[3] "Moral goodness" often had more to do with religion and social norms than it did logic and ethical principles, which led to subjective explanations as to why certain things should or should not be done.

---

1   Murphy par. 1
2   Halsall 1
3   Paxman 47

The advent of progressive philosophers like Thomas Hobbes, Samuel Clarke, Lord Ashley Shaftesbury, and Francis Hutcheson revolutionized the ideals presented in conduct books accordingly. Hobbes's 1651 *Leviathan* enforced the ethical necessity for strong government and laws by arguing that humans in their natural state lead "nasty, brutish, and short" lives. This authoritarian perspective was reflected in later conduct books. Clarke advanced the idea of rationalist ethics in criticism of Hobbes, stating that natural truths were implicit in religion and could be proven so through the use of reason. In addition, Shaftesbury and Hutcheson advocated for the moral sense that recognized and approved of virtuous behavior.[4] The application of these theories by different authors further broadened the scope of what society considered "ideal behavior."

As a general rule, conduct books were geared more towards girls because there was a higher expectation of propriety and a more strict social code for women than for men. Although some contained sections for different ages, sexes, and classes, the majority of conduct books provided advice on female behavior. One such example is *A Father's Legacy to His Daughters*, written in 1777 by Dr. Gregory of Edinburgh: it contains chapters on Religion, Conduct and Behavior, Amusements, and Friendship, Love, and Marriage. These chapters outlined guidance for each of the categories and how to act appropriately with regards to each of them.

One assumption present in most mid-eighteenth century conduct books was that the audience, older children approaching adulthood, had no other guiding forces; that is, they lacked living parents or guardians. This marked a transition from conduct books as directions from an expert to a replacement for a living mentor. Thus, the tone of conduct books became less lofty than was previously common and traded strict authority for encouragement and a holistic approach to managing oneself through adolescence.[1] In some cases, there was an element of truth in writing to orphans, as in *A Father's Legacy to His Daughters*. Gregory wrote it as he grew ill, knowing that he would not be alive to raise his daughters (his wife had passed away some years previously). It was published posthumously and became popular shortly thereafter. Conduct book authors were, in many cases, driven by a sense of responsibility to ensure that the next generation would have a morally correct mentor.

Writing letters from the rhetorical perspective of the dead was also a common and powerful device. The advantage of employing this fiction to give advice is that its counsel was thought to be infinitely wise and all-knowing—the dead could look into the past with understanding as well as interpret present events. Guidance from the grave could also be tailored to fit a story that would carry weight with its readers and overcome any indifference that could arise from reading a dry volume of rules and direction from some faraway scholar. Imagining the author to be a benevolent source of wisdom who has bypassed the bonds of death in order to impart a message was often an effective method of keeping the reader's attention.[2] Such letters from the dead provide a dynamic and judicious guardian figure and model both proper conduct and good writing communication.

---

1   Paxman 38
2   Paxman 53-55

Sodomy

The roles of men associated with sodomy underwent a transition during the late 1600s to early 1700s.[3] At first, most sodomites were believed to be masculine in dress and mannerisms. The political implications of sodomy were such that men who were libertines and republicans had a greater proclivity to homosexuality. However, the boundaries between sodomy and effeminacy blurred and brought the issue more clearly into the public eye as awareness increased.

Around 1710, the male devolved into two different roles: the natural man and the molly, an effeminate sodomite. The natural man would be exclusively attracted to women throughout the entirety of his life and would never behave in a feminine manner, whereas the molly characterized male and female qualities equally. He would, although physically male, be considered to be half of the worst type of woman: a prostitute. In addition, his attraction would lie only in men despite his tendency to marry a woman as a safeguard from public censure. The idea that there were three genders—male, female, and sodomite—was likely brought about by the increase in gender equality in modern northwestern European countries. The terms "molly" and "gay" were the most frequently used in description of homosexual males. Molly in particular was used for over one hundred and fifty years and was in use longer than today's term "homosexual."[4]

The first law prohibiting sodomy was the Statute of 1533, issued by Henry VIII as a civil offense punishable by death. Laws regarding sodomy were numerous, but most often convictions were for "assault with sodomitical intent"

---

3   Trumbach 105
4   Trumbach 106

rather than actual sodomy. The reason for this was that to convict a man of sodomy, there had to be two witnesses to prove that both penetration (oral or anal) and ejaculation occurred. Either partner could be found guilty in most situations. In the majority of cases, the penalty was death.[1] As laws became less harsh, men were increasingly sent to the pillory and pelted with an assortment of rotting vegetables, dead cats, and slaughterhouse refuse. By the early 1800s, most cases were classified as felonies and penalized by imprisonment, although it endured as a capital offense until 1828 in England.[2]

In the middle of the eighteenth century, the role of the beau was popularized in England by men who wished to embody the spirit of the old-fashioned rake with foppish tendencies. Whereas "fop" was a derogatory term associated with effeminate dress, "beau" was a self-describing word for a man who took great pains to perfect his appearance and dress. Along with this term came the practice of sodomizing young boys.[3] The first documented case of associating feminine dress with sodomy occurred in the 1698 sodomy trial for Captain Rigby, a beau who had tried to seduce a young boy in a public park. During the trial, one of his critics said that his "effeminate madness" was to blame for his taste for sodomy—his clothes were feminine in style, and he had been accused of wearing petticoats.[4]

The beginning of the eighteenth century also marked an increase in the belief that sex was not only a biological function, but that its moral implications led to genetic consequences; that is to say, if one were to have what was considered a sexual

1   Emsley, Hitchcock, and Shoemaker par. 4
2   "Homosexuality and the Law in England" par. 1
3   Trumbach 107
4   Trumbach 108

perversion (such as homosexuality), one's genealogy could be traced back to an ancestor with some entirely unrelated physical or mental malady. Similarly, "heredity" would dictate that the sexual perversion be present in one's descendants in the form of sterility or other medical conditions.[5] The prevalence of this idea made sodomy an even graver crime. Not only was it illegal, it was also considered to be a disorder in itself and would harm one's family in future generations.

Despite its legal and supposed medical ramifications, in the early 1700s the gay subculture was thriving in England, marking the first time in history that gay men gathered together in social organizations and created a network of communication among themselves. Gay clubs, called "molly houses," were more numerous in the 1720s than in the 1950s when Parliament began to consider revising laws that pertained to homosexuality. There is some speculation as to why the gay subculture arose when it did, but it can mostly be attributed to urbanization. The large population had a correspondingly larger number of homosexual men, thus providing sufficient people and anonymity to create a subculture in London; the population in 1725 was estimated to be about 750,000. The infamy of molly houses ensured their popularity as soon as they sprang up across London. The gay subculture would later become less visible, but when it first began it existed in full view of the rest of the world. The attention given to the movement by those who condemned it, ironically, served to unite it and bring a definitive gay community together.[6]

---

5   Foucault 118
6   Norton *Mother Clap's Molly House* 10

The Game of Flatts

The term "lesbian" did not yet exist during the eighteenth century, and the idea that sexual acts occurred between women was just beginning to enter into public awareness. "The Game of Flatts" described the physical act of women rubbing their "flat" genitalia together. In Europe, sexuality was considered phallocentric—a woman could be attracted to a man and a man could be attracted to a man, but women lacked the ability to sexually please each other.[1] Legal consequences for women accused of doing the Game of Flatts were inconsistent, for awareness of the act was so new that laws did not yet exist to outlaw it or mete out punishment for it. In most cases, it was treated much the same as sodomy in a court of law. Laws that did exist for homosexuality, such as the English Act of 1533, did not specifically mention women despite detailing different situations and specifics of sodomy.[2]

The mention of the Game of Flatts in *Satan's Harvest Home* is curious because, although people knew it existed at some level, it was not in the general public consciousness during the 1700s. From the earliest days of the church, homosexuality between women was believed to exist because "God being angry with the human race because of their idolatry, it came about that a woman would desire a woman for the use of foul lust." This was an interpretation of Romans (1:26) by Saint Ambrose regarding the "vile affections" of women and considered all the more offensive because women were supposed to have a greater sense of modesty. The Game of Flatts was included in most penance manuals as part of the list of sins a clergy could potentially encounter. In matters of law,

1   Brown 67
2   Norton "The Buggery Statute" par. 1

however, sex between women only accounted for a handful of the thousands of total trials for sodomy. There were a few in Spain and eight total others across France, Germany, Switzerland, and Italy.[3]

Lacking in documented cases but being a strong source of ecclesiastical censure, it is difficult to say exactly how common eighteenth century lesbianism was. Whereas the gay male subculture was widely prevalent in Europe, lesbian subculture did not exist until over one hundred years later. This can be attributed to the sexual oppression of women and the medicalization of their sex. Virginity was sacred and its protection of utmost importance; especially in the aristocracy, the pathology of sex was emphasized in girls' upbringings and any behaviors suggesting immodesty were closely monitored and corrected. The secrecy and taboo nature of heterosexual sex increased exponentially in relation to sex between women; in contrast to sodomy, it was almost unmentionable. Sex that occurred without a man was a foreign concept that inspired "an almost active willingness to *dis*believe," as evidenced by the glacial pace at which public awareness and laws developed.[4] People were suspicious of lesbian activities, but more often it went unacknowledged; for example, it was forbidden for nuns to lock their doors or sleep in the same cell together, and they were required to leave a lamp lit through the night. There were no explanations as to what activities these rules were intended to prevent, but it does not seem a far stretch to postulate that the church was suspicious of nuns partaking in the Game of Flatts.

As lesbianism gained more attention, it became common for authors to address it as an activity of young women and

3   Brown 68
4   Brown 69

widows as a safer alternative to sex with men— they could curb their sexual appetites with each other without risking pregnancy or loss of virginity. Inherent in this viewpoint was the notion that lesbian sex was not a replacement for heterosexual sex; rather, it was a temporary exercise to "practice" for sex with men. By thus labelling the Game of Flatts merely a means of preparing for or elevating heterosexual sex, lesbianism was made harmless to ignore. Another hypothesis was that, being the naturally weaker and more degenerate sex, women were trying to embody a man's valor and honor by seducing another woman. Unlike the first justification, this did not pardon sex between women. However, it may have been partially responsible for the Western convention of women attempting to perfect themselves by overcoming their feminine weakness.[1]

For the most part, authors who addressed the Game of Flatts in eighteenth century writing tended to be more accepting of lesbian sex than of male sodomy. The penance for sex between women was, as prescribed by Theodore of Tarsus, three years: the same sentence as "solitary vice." Sex between men could only be recompensed by ten years of penance. Similarly, Gregory III's accord suggested one hundred sixty days of penance for homosexual women but a year or more for homosexual men. According to Charles Borromeo's penitential, the penalty for two women "fornicating" was two years (the same penance was required if she did so alone), whereas for two men the atonement ranged from seven to fifteen years depending on marital status. More leniency towards women was generally the trend, but there were several exceptions, particularly as more laws were developed. Some advocated for equal punishment of homosexuality in men and women, others offered

1   Brown 71

a series of conditions under which different punishments were prescribed (i.e., the use of a "material instrument" versus sex "only by rubbing" would have different degrees of penance), and harsh ones recommended hanging or burning.[2]

***

Hell Upon Earth and *Satan's Harvest Home* were penned at a time of growing awareness and censure of same-sex desire. These two anonymous texts represent important voices from the past that help us better understand the complex relationship between desire, sexual behavior, and propriety in eighteenth century England. Long available only in facsimile, the two works appear here in an affordable typeset edition for the first time in recent history.

2   Brown 72

Bibliography

Brown, Judith. "Lesbian Sexuality in Medieval and Early Modern Europe." *Hidden from History: Reclaiming the Gay and Lesbian Past.* Ed. Martin Duberman, Martha Vicinus, and George Chauncey Jr. New York: Meridian, 1989. 67-75. Print.

Emsley, Clive, Tim Hitchcock, and Robert Shoemaker. "Communities - Homosexuality. *The Proceedings of the Old Bailey.* N.p, n.d. Web. 20 March 2016.

Focault, Michel. The History of Sexuality. New York: Random House, Inc., 1980. Print.

Halsall, Paul. "Ancient History Sourcebook: The Precepts of Ptah-Hotep, C. 2200 BCE." *Internet History Sourcebooks.* Fordham University, n.d. Web. 20 May 2016.

"Homosexuality and the Law in England." *Wilde Law Page.* University of Missouri-Kansas City, n.d. Web. 20 Mar. 2016.

Murphy, Terence R. "Conduct Books - Oxford Reference." *Conduct Books.* Oxford Reference, n.d. Web. 20 Mar. 2016.

Norton, Rictor. "The Buggery Statute." *Homosexuality in Eighteenth-Century England: A Sourcebook.* N.p., 10 Jan. 2016. Web. 20 Mar. 2016.

Norton, Rictor. *Mother Clap's Molly House: The Gay Subculture in England 1700-1830.* London: GMP Publishers Ltd, 1992. Print.

Paxman, David B. "The Mentor's Anxiety: Conduct Books and the Proliferation of Virtuous Guidance." *Religion in the Age of Enlightenment* 1 (2009): 33-57. Print.

Thomas, Hobbes. "Hobbes's Leviathan: Reprinted from the Edition of 1651 : Hobbes, Thomas, 1588-1679 : Free Download & Streaming : Internet Archive." *Internet Archive*. Oxford: Clarendon Press, n.d. Web. 20 Mar. 2016.

Trumbach, Randolph. "The Birth of the Queen: Sodomy and the Emergence of Gender Equality in Modern Culture, 1660-1750. *Hidden from History: Reclaiming the Gay and Lesbian Past.* Ed. Martin Duberman, Martha Vicinus, and George Chauncey Jr. New York: Meridian, 1989. 129-140. Print.

Yenter, Timothy. "Samuel Clarke." *Stanford University*. Stanford University, 05 Apr. 2003. Web. 20 Mar. 2016.

HELL upon EARTH:
OR THE
Town in an Uproar.
OCCASION'D BY

The late horrible Scenes of Forgery, Perjury, Street-Robbery, Murder, Sodomy, and other shocking Impieties. Of the Encrease of the Hempen Manufactory and the Degrease of the Woollen Manufactory; shewing that Goals and Gibbets are become as useful as Guards and Garisons, and Pillories as necessary as P——ns.

Of Peoples being almost under the Necessity of carrying Pistols instead of Prayer-books to their Parish Churches.

A surprising Account of the Numbers of People who *Lie* by preparing and vending Liquors, and of those that *Die* by drinking them: With the vast plenty of Diseases and Doctors, and the great Scarcity of Physicians.

An Account of Fox-Hunters, Peace-Hunters, Money-Hunters, Men-Hunters, Whore-Hunters, Death-Hunters, Levee-Hunters, News-Hunters.

Of the Subscribing Coffee-Mens petty Project for printing their Customers Prittle Prattle.

Of Lady *B——ts* Necessary House being broke open and robb'd, as published in the Coffee-mens Paper, with the strange Effect it has on a *Scotch* Subscribing Coffee-man's Wife, who refunded her Breakfast upon reading the Relation.

LONDON:

Printed for J. ROBERTS in *Warwick-Lane*,
and A. DODD without *Temple-Bar*, 1729.

(Price One Shilling.)

Hell upon Earth

THIS great, wicked, unwieldy, over-grown Town, one continued hurry of Vice and Pleasure; where nothing dwells but *Absurdities, Abuses, Accidents, Accusations, Admirations, Adventures, Adversities, Advertisements, Adulteries, Affidavits, Affectations, Affirmations, Afflictions, Affronts, Aggravations, Agitations, Agonies, Airs, Alarms, Ailments, Allurements, Alterations, Ambitions, Amours, Ampitheatres, Anathemas, Animosities, Anxieties, Appointments, Apprehensions, Arrests, Arrogances, Assassinations, Assemblies, Assessments, Assurances, Assignations, Attainders, Audacities, Aversions, &c.*

The usual Observations of the SABBATH *in the good Cities of* London *and* Westminster, *and Parts adjacent.*

SUNDAY. *Six in the Morning.*
Coaches, Chaises, Chairs, Phaetons, and Hackney Horses harnessing and getting ready for Citizens and their Wives, Doxies and Daughters. — Lascivious Gentlemen and Tradesmen stealing from their Maid Servants Garrets to their own Bed-Chambers. — *Irishmen* meditating to the Destruction of Maids, Wives, Widows and Trades-People on their Pillows. — Infirm and superannuated Letchers plagued in their Beds with impracticable *Desires*. — News-Mongers *inventing* Stories of Rapes, Riots, Robberies, &c. for their next Papers. — Obscurity, Flatness and Impertinency flowing in upon the Meditations of certain Poetasters.

Seven o'Clock.

Young Officers of the Army, and the Navy, Doctors-Commons-Men, Lawyers Clerks, and Mercers Journeymen, *cum multis Aliis*, taking their *Mercurials* and *Water-Gruel.* — Servant Wenches pilfering their Mistresses *Teas* and *Sugars* to entertain their Visitants in the Afternoon. —Half-Pay Officers Laundresses scolding and refusing to deliver their Linnen without *ready Money.* — Beggars, Apple-Women, and Shoe-Blackers repairing to their respective Stands. — *Demi-Clergymen,* alias *Parish-Clerks*, putting on their Brands and grave Countenances.

Eight o'Clock.

Lawyers in the Inns of Court lacing their Mistresses Stays, paying them their *Fees*, and removing them by *Habeas Corpus* to their own Lodgings. — Bawds with *Bandboxes* running to Mens Wives and Daughters to manage Intrigues for the Evening. — Ladies Lap-Dogs cleaning and dressing to accompany their Mistresses to Church. — Apothecaries with their 'Prentices trotting thro' the Streets with Pills, Purges and Potions. — Clear-Starchers, Manteau-Makers Journey-Women, Servants out of Place, and poor harlots running upon *Tick* at Chandlers Shops for Tea and Coffee. — Barbers as busy as *Newgate* Sollicitors at an *Old Baily* Sessions in embellishing their Customers.

Nine o'Clock.

Vintners Wives brawling and exercising their Lungs upon their Servants in their Kitchens. — *Fleet*-Parsons at their Stations on *Ludgate-Hill*, looking out sharp for *Weddings* from *White-Chapel* and *Wapping.* — City 'Prentices dressed spruce at their Masters Doors, appointing their Afternoons Rambles. — Involvement Debtors appear out of the *Verge* of the Court with gay Countenances. — Informers begin to be in Motion in the Streets. — Physicians poring over Books as they ride thro' the Town in their Chariots, to give the World a Sense of their *Religion* and *deep Study.* — Whores hurrying home in Hackney-Coaches from Bagnios to shift their Linnen. — Taylors and Perriwig-makers uttering great Numbers of *Lies* to their Customers by commending their Airs, Shapes, Mien, *&c.* — People busy in erasing out of their wearing *Apparel* the *Wrinkles* and other *Symptoms* of their having been under *Date* and *Tribulation* at the Pawnbrokers.

Ten o'Clock.

Noblemens and Gentlemens Doors free from Duns. — Young *Milliners* and *Sempstresses* as lazy in their Beds as *Life-Guardsmen* in their Quarters. — People of Quality's Chamber-Bells ringing for their *Valets* and *Abigails.* — Church-wardens, Overseers, and other Parochial Officers, proceeding to Church with their Families rather for form sake than Devotion. — Rakes of Quality and young Students in the Inns of Court humming over *Opera* Tunes in their Chambers. — Hackney Writers, Poets, and *Welch* Sollicitors *cogging* their Stockings and *dearning* their Shirt Collars in order to issue forth from their Garrets to borrow half a Crown or beg a Dinner. — Smutty Jests, loud Laughter, and some Scandal, going forward at *Ladies* Tea Tables.

Eleven o'Clock.

Fine Fans, rich Brilliants, white Hands, envious Eyes, and gold Snuff-Boxes displaying in all Parish Churches. — Many excellent *stolen* Sermons preaching by some Clergymen who won't take Pains to make worse of their *Own.* — Folks of *Fashion* humbling themselves in *Tissue Cloth,* and *rich Laces*, and enduring the *fatigue* of Divine Service with wonderful seeming Patience. — Drunken Beggars battling and breaking one anothers Heads about the Streets in dividing the *Charity* of ostentatious Fools and old Women. — Hackney *Coachmen* and *Chairmen* lifting up their Eyes towards Heaven for *wet Weather.* — Jacks, *Spits*, and *Porridge-Pots* all in Motion in the Cities of *London* and *Westminster*, and Parts adjacent. — Dabs of Beef, Pork, and Mutton, roasting in *Packthread Strings* in the Garrets of married *Coblers, Porters,* and *Penny-Postmen.*

Twelve at Noon.

All of the *Religions* within the Weekly Bills of Mortality return'd by their respective Teachers on the Hands of the several Parishes they belong to. — Citizens Wives, some at their Dram Bottles, and others criticising upon one another's Dress and Behaviours at Church, and throwing out little Portions of Slander as a whet before Dinner. — Young Tradesmen, Takes, and Lawyers-Clerks, *fuddling* and very noisy in Tavern Kitchens. — Ladies about St. *James's* and *Hanover-Square*, reading *Plays* and *Novels*, and making mundifying Washes. — Begging Cripples in the Streets bestowing Prayers and Benedictions on their Benefactors. — Hackney Coaches running from *Westminster* to *Wapping, &c.* cramm'd with Men, Women, and Children, going to Diner with their Friends and Relations. — Poets and Philosophers in Motion about *Gray's-Inn-Walks* and St. *James's-Park*, wrapt up in Thread-bare coats, Study and Speculation. — Innocent People of more Merit than Fortune, sitting down to homely wholesome Food with *Calm Consciences.* — All the common People's *Jaws* in and round this great Metropolis in full *Employment.* — Bakers and Pastry-Cooks running thro' the Streets with *Puddings* and *Pies* that have suffered some *Abridgment* in their Houses.

Two o'Clock

Victuallers and their Wives busy in making *Punch* with their worst Brandy for the Guests they have entertain'd at *Dinner.* — *Learned* Dissertations upon the *Craftsman* and *Fogg, Figg's Ampitheatre, Proceedings* at the *Old Baily,* &c. going forward in ale-house Conversations. — Vintners Wives *ogling* and stealing *Looks* at their gay Customers as they sit together at Dinner behind the Bar. — Church-Bells and Taverns-Bells keeping *Time* with one another.

Three o'Clock.

Young handsome Wenches in Churches demanding Adoration instead of paying it. — Shoals of Servant Maids and straggling Apprentices crowding into the Cathedrals of St. *Paul's London*, and St. *Peter's Westminster*, to hear the Musick, and when the Anthem is over, sneak away. — Coachmen, Footmen, and Chairmen, all in an Uproar about St. *James's Palace.* — City Tradesmen with *full Bellies* and *empty Minds*, gaping at the Nobility and Quality as they pass from the Court. — The Fortunate and Great sitting down to Meals of Pomp and Ceremony, attended by sumptuous side-Boards, Sycophants, and little Sincerity. — Certain Citizens and their Wives retiring to their *Couches.* — The *walking Gentry* drove into Churches *Nolens Volens* to escape the Wrath of a *Shower* rather than that of Divine *Vengeance.*

Four o'Clock.

Certain Ladies of Quality at *Quadrille, Ombre,* &c. — A general *Jumble* and *Jostle* from *White-Chapel* to *Charing-Cross*, of Country Juggs, Barbers 'Prentices, Tavern Drawers, Men and their Wives, Women and their Husbands, Children, *&c.* — Drunken Bullies, Beaus, and Gamesters, *Religiously* in their Beds as remembering the *Sabbath* was appointed for a Day of Rest. —Footmen, Journeymen, and Apprentices, engag'd in low Amours in Gentlemens and Shopkeepers *Kitchens*. — Handicraft Tradesmen matching to and from *Islington* and *Chelsea*, with their Offspring in their Arms, followed by their Wives, chearfully bearing the Ensigns of their Duty and Obedience, *viz.* their Husbands Canes.

Five o'Clock.

Half-Pay Officers, poor Clerks in the Offices, Drapers Journeymen, and *Gentlemen* of the *sixth Rate* Popping into Pale Alehouses. — Seditious Discourses going forward in certain Jacobite Coffee-houses, and other private Publick-houses in the dark Corners of the Town. — Men, Women and Children, returning into Town from the Fields as hungry as *Hugonots* newly landed from *Callais*. — Women at their Tea Tables sitting like Coroners Inquests upon the murdered Reputations of their Neighbours. — A general Chit-Chat, tittle-tattle, admiring and commending, approving and disapproving of Womens Dresses, their Manteau-Makers, Milliners, *&c.*

Six o'Clock.

Hired Servants got together railing at, and reviling the Families that entertain them, and advancing the old Doctrine of there being *more Places than Parish Churches.* — Sober Families going to Evening-Lectures, or performing religious Duties at home. — Pick Pockets following to rob them. — Rakes and Reprobates running into Bawdy-Houses and Taverns. — Foot Soldiers drunk with Geneva. — People of Qualities Servants just got to Dinner. — 'Prentices prattling Politicks in tipling Houses. — Drunken Christenings and Funerals going forward at St. *Giles's in the Fields, Stepney* and *Cripplegate* Parishes, *&c.*

Seven o'Clock.

The celebrated Mother *H—y—d* Cursing, Rending, and Roaring at her Maids and Drawers, to drown the Cries and Groans of *departing Maidenheads.* — Coffee-houses crowded with powder'd Fops. — Scarce one third of the common People sober. — Pamper'd Footmen and Flambeaux flying before the Coaches and Chairs of visiting Ladies at the Court End of the Town.

Eight o'Clock.

The principal Streets fill'd with *Whores, Shoe-makers, Butchers, Joiners,* and all sorts of Handicraft Tradesmen passing and repassing one another. — 'Prentices and their Sweethearts taking their parting Kisses. — Lady *B——*, Cursing or Praying, according to the run of the Dice.

Nine o'Clock.

Drunken Quarrels at all Corners of the Streets amongst the Mob about Precedency. — Poor Wretches packing up their wearing Apparel to return them early next Morning in to the Hands of the Pawnbrokers. — Children, Servants, old Women, and others of the same size of Understanding, pleasing and terrifying themselves and one another with Stories of Witches, Devils and Apparitions.

The various kinds of MURTHER which are daily perpetrated in this Town, has given the considering part of Mankind much Concern; for if we look back but a short time, we see what dreadful Havock the *Pestle* has made amongst us, and what Numbers still continue to perish weekly by *Prescription.* But while one part of the Creation falls by the Hands of *Others,* another part generously falls by their *Own*: These fit every Morning and Evening in Taverns and Ale-houses, ringing their own *Passing Bell* in Peace and Pleasure.

The last War was so abstemious as not to devour above half a score Thousand of our Countrymen in a whole Campaign; but what is that to the Triumphs of *Physick* and the *Bottle*, within the Bills of Mortality, which are abundantly illustrated in those elegant *Weekly Records* composed to the Honour of *Esculapius*, and sung or said by the Company of Parish Clerks in and round this Metropolis.

A *Physician* may as soon be brought to *Faith* and *Repentance*, or a *Jew* to *Continence,* as a Person of Business that is obliged to be much abroad in this Town, to live a regular sober Life in it; besides the Crowds of Acquaintances and Importunities he is liable to meet with; the Vintners, Victuallers, and Coffee-house Men, are eternally upon the *Watch* at their Doors and Windows, *hemming* after every one that passes, to make Tippling Matches, and propagate the Doctrine of Drinking.

Moreover the vast Preparations we daily see making for setting up more Taverns, Coffee-houses, and Tippling-houses, as if the Island had suffered some wonderful Change in its Clime, was remov'd under the *Torrid Zone*, and some strange and natural *Drought* had seiz'd the Spirits of the People. In short their Number is already so exceeding great, that to the Honour of the Nation be is spoken, no City in the Universe can boast of so handsome a show of *Bushes, Bacchus's, Lattices,* and *Stills,* as our Metropolis.

How many of his Majesties Liege Subjects are drown'd every Year in Seas of *Wine*, *Welch* Ale, and *October*? And how many Ladies at twenty five declare for Brandy and Arrack Punch, and so leave Posterity to shift for it self, for truly they'll breed no more?

A poor limber-back'd Beau at the Court End of the Town, rarely holds it out above two or three Years, and a Whetter about the Royal Exchange as much longer, while a fat overgrown Parish Officer may make a shift to serve a dozen Years Apprenticeship to Swallowing; for having as much Flesh and small Spirit, he is a long time a wasting, even as a great Candle with a little Wick, will yield a dim and stupid Light for a long while together, and yet consume it self in the End.

We had a late notable Instance how detestable this Vice begins to appear in the Eyes of the Army, upon which I congratulate the Military part of my Countrymen; and that was, when a Noble Lord, greatly *disguised* in *Wine,* was endeavouring to pass through St. *James*'s *Park*, the commanding Officer, who was an *Irishman*, insisted upon the Letter of his Orders, to suffer no Person whatsoever to pass with a *Load*, and turn'd his Lordship out at the Gate accordingly.

The present detection of Morals, and likewise our want of People, I cannot altogether lay at the Door of the above-mention'd Vice, but in a great measure to the unreasonable GALLANTRIES now going forward amongst us. Have we scarce had a Marriage of any Consequence in the Town for a Twelve-month: Are not the publick Papers filled with *Elopements* of Wives and young Wenches, and a common Proverb verified; *That a* Middlesex *Maidenhead is to be had for asking for.* A few Years ago our Rakes of Quality used to commit Matrimony as they did Murther, out of a Frolick, and were ready to hang themselves for it the next Day; for we had an Instance of a *fashionable Pair*, who for many Months after Marriage would never be brought to agree but in one thing, which was, to *separate for ever.*

Indeed at St. *Pancrass* and the *Fleet*, where Marriages are retailed at *reasonable* Rates, there shall be such *coupling* of Beggars on a *Sunday* Morning, that they stand behind one another, as it were in a Country Dance; but what Benefit the Publick receives from such Alliances, I shall leave the Officers of Parishes to describe. A Man now-a-Days is hardly reproach-able that deludes an innocent Woman, though she has never so much *Merit*; if she is below him in Fortune, the Man has no Dishonour following his Treachery; and her own Sex are so debased by Custom, as to say in the Case of the Woman: *How could she expect he would marry her.*

I am inclined to believe, that the *Seventh Commandment* ought to be kept, but I am wond'rous loth to declare so much to the World, for fear of angering *Folks of Fashion*; and there-fore to keep Measures with the Quality and my own Con-science, I do hereby signify to all my loving Readers, that in *Persons of Figure*, the Breaches of their marriage *Vow* and In-fidelity to their Yoke-Mates, is not Adultery, but something very like it. In the Man it is but *taking of a Wench*, and in the married Ladies 'tis only a *piece of Gallantry.* Now when this Sin is Christened with such modish pretty Names, it frightens no Body; on the contrary, it becomes even an innocent and reputable thing.

As I am a publick Spirited Person, and have at Heart the good of my Country, as does in some Measure appear by this humble Essay, I have been long of Opinion, that noth-ing can be more reasonable than to permit the DAMNERS, and SINKERS to lend their Assistance, to add to the *sinking* Fund of the Nation: In order to which, I hope the following Scheme will neither be thought extravagant nor impractica-ble.

Imprimis, That for every single *Curse*, exhibited by a Man or Woman of Quality, during their Dressing-time, there be imposed a Fine of *One Shilling.*

For every *Curse* in the Guard-Rooms at St. *James*'s and the *Tilt-Yard, One Penny*; and because this, by some may be thought too weighty a Burthen on the Gentlemen of the

Army in a time of Peace, as well an Infringement on their antient *Rights* and *Priviledges*, I submit it entirely to my Superiors to mitigate it in such Manner, as to them in their great Wisdom shall seem meet.

For every *Curse* of the principal Commander, or inferior Officer of any Ship of Force or Burthen, during the time of an Engagement, Storm, or other imminent Danger, *One Shilling.*

For every single *Curse* of a *Counseller, Sollicitor, Petty-fogger, Bailiff*, together with every other collateral Branch of the Law, *Eight Pence*; unless such, can make it appear by the Oath of one or more credible Witnesses, that he or they, have within the space of twelve Calendar Months, once rehears'd the *Lord's Prayer*, or appeared within the Walls of a Church, for any other Purpose than to attend a Funeral, and Intrigue, or to shun a *Shower*, then, to plead the General Issue, and give the special Matter in Evidence in Bar of the Penalty contain'd in this Article.

For every *Oath* voided by the Countess of *B*——— when her Ladyship loses at Ombre, *Two Shillings*, except such Oath be an Original, and of her own composing.

For all *Oaths* at the Groom-porters, and at Horse-Racing, Prize-fighting, and Cocking, *One Shilling* and *Six Pence* each.

A Person losing a Cause either in Law or Equity, for each *Oath* thereupon *Eight Pence*.

For every *Oath* of a disappointed *Dunner* on a *Saturday Six Pence.*

All Persons crossed and disappointed in Love, for every *Oath, ditto.*

For every *Curse* uttered by the Buyer of a Bear in *Exchange-Alley, Six Pence*, provided always that this shall not extend to any Purchaser in the *Welch-Copper* and *York-Buildings.*

Provided always that nothing herein contained shall be construed to extend to deprive the Beaus at *Buttons* and the *Tilt-Yard*, of the benefit of that terrible Term, *Death*, or of any other useful Expletive, such as *Blood, Hell*, and that excellent *English* Particle *Zounds*, which comprehends so much of the Beauty of our Language, and which is so much received and applauded; all which compose a very graceful Parenthesis, and supply any Hesitation, in the Utterance or Chasme in the Sense, with great Success.

There is a LEVELLING PRINCIPLE in humane Nature, by which all Men are animated to pull down to their own Pitch, or below it, every one who by good fortune or Capacity has got above them. Those whom we cannot overtake we abuse, and by railing at Merit make our own want of it more conspicuous. Though this vile Impulse to Slander, with which we True-Born *Englishmen* are so richly levened, has it not in its Power to lessen or destroy those excellent Qualities that provoke it, yet it has frequently the cursed Success to marr their Operation, and render them useless by depreciating them continually, and deforming them with filthy Colours, and gaining daily Proselytes to its *Lies*.

I have known such monstrous *Lies* rais'd against a Minister of State, that would have drawn Blushes from the Cheeks of a Bawd, or Modesty from the Countenance of an *Exchange* Broker, for no other Reason, but that he hath fill'd his Place with vast Sufficiency and Honour, and even on an assured Confidence of his having had Goodness and Temper enough to *forgive* the Libellers. Nay the Sacred Person of MAJESTY it self has not escap'd this sort of Calumny; and so catching is this base Spirit, that let but a little snarling Cur in a Corner begin the Bark, and it shall in an Instant be handed, or rather mouth'd about by all the Beagles of the same Kidney.

With what Confidence and Industry had we some late ridiculous Reports of *Changes* in this Administration sent through the Kingdom. The *Tripoli* Embassador was complimented on his being made Master of the Horse; and a *Bishop* had the Drums and Musick before his Door for being appointed Pay-master of the Forces. The Command of the Army was given to Boys and Girls: In short we had not a Statesman or a Soldier who was not *lied* out of his Employment.

I have heard a Company of City Apprentices talk as pertly of Affairs pretended to be transacted in Council, as if they had been at the Board and taken Minutes.

A *Roman Catholick* Gentleman called to me one Day on *Duke Humphrey's Walk* in the *Park*, and ask'd if I had not heard of the two Dozen of *Expresses* that had brought the News of the Plenipotentiaries breaking up the Congress and one anothers Heads, and running away from *Soissons.*

The *Fr——h* Embassador has been packing up his Goods every Day these *two Years* to leave the Kingdom on a *sudden* and in *Disgust*: and our Minister at *Paris* has been as oftentimes *recalled.*

I was told of an honest Country Gentleman, a constant Reader and Admirer of *Mist* and the *Craftsman*, who had ne'er seen the Town, and was coming to it the other Day from *Oxfordshire* on his private Affairs, had been so blinded and infatuated with this sort of *Intelligence,* that passing through the Town of *Uxbridge*, where a Troop of the Royal Blue Guards being drawn up, with their Belts in the form of a *Cross* on their Backs and Breasts, he took them to be part of the *Spanish* Army, and escap'd in a most terrible Fright back to his Family.

To CENSURE and be CENSUR'D, is the portion of the FAIR SEX, which they freely deal to each; insomuch that a Propensity to Back-bite is become absolutely necessary to Self-defence; for as every one of them is abused by the rest, it is but just that every one of them should have her Regence by abusing the rest in their turn. Hence I would in their Favour infer, that when one Lady stabs the Reputation of another, tho' ever so mortally, yet the same must not be construed into Murder, but only be deemed *Woman Slaughter*, and committed *se defendendo*: and indeed, if the whole Sex were by general Consent to kill one another's Credit in this manner at all Adventures, the Crime would still endure the like Mitigation. I grant there are some Women not so well qualified in the Art of Reviling: But then the default lies in this, that either their Tongues are not so quick, which seldom happens, or their invention is slow, which is as great a Rarity; for if we peep into their Hearts and Inventions, we shall generally find them upon a Par with their more eloquent Sisters in the Trade and Mystery of Scandal: Though there be some of the Sex that are but Dabblers, a vast Majority are wonderful Proficients. I do not pretend to debar the Ladies from dear Gratification of Scandal; I would only beg them to turn it into another Channel, in which it might run with less Mischief and Danger to themselves. As the same Dirt which they throw is for the most part thrown upon them, they ought for their own sakes, since they must be dealing in Slander, to say only things that are galling, and not things that are quite killing, which is the common Practice. Instead of saying, *Such a one is no better than she should be*; let them say, *she is a Slattern*, and knows nothing of Dress. For though this dreadful Charge may be to her worse than the former, and far more unpardonable, yet her Husband and Children may live in good Credit, notwithstanding one side of her Gown hangs deeper than t'other. I am afraid this Advice of mine will not go down with 'em, though it is evidently for their Advantage. It is a hard matter, if not utterly impossible, to find *one good Woman* in the Town who will allow that there is *another good*

Woman in it. She assures herself, either from Breeding, Spite, or *Experience*, that they are all very bad, and therefore resolves to give no Quarter. Thus when her Opinion and her Passion meet, and she Acts both from *Belief* and *Desire*, what can stand before her? And yet if any of her Sister Females shew that they have feeling and strike again, or having the same Opinion of her which she has of them, treat her in the same mrnner, *she is Bely'd, and Wrong'd, and Innocent*, and the Lord knows what. Thus the harmless injured Creature seeks Abuse by giving it, and then laments that she is repaid.

There is a VANITY incident to Men in every degree and station of Life; from the highest to the lowest; every Person aims at establishing a Reputation, and excelling others of his Profession; from the Prince to the Peasant, from the Court to the Dunghil this Vanity does prevail: But most Persons have indeed so weak a Foundation to build upon, their Reputation totters and falls to the Ground before they can raise it to the heighth of their Wishes: And if we were to examine into the conduct of the several Pretenders, we should find the true Reasons to be occasioned by an irregular Pursuit of those Honours they aim at.

Thus we see the Malcontent would be recorded for his Loyalty, notwithstanding he is always thwarting and opposing the Interest of his Prince, and thinks he has Injustice done him if any should dispute his Merits.

He who sets up for a Politician, would be thought the most profound in those Mysteries, upon no better Score than that of a Vociferous Qualification, and a particular Faulty of continually swimming against the Stream.

The Churchman, who either from a want of Learning or Indolence, has scarcely attain'd the Advantage of a Collegiate Education; upon the Merits of his Cloth only, claims the Title of an eminent Divine, and holds it a Crime in the Laity equal to Sacrilege to question his Pretentions thereto.

The meanest Empirick in the Kingdom would fain have you think him a graduate Physician, and his own Modesty sets him upon an Equality with a *Radcliff*, a *Friend*, or a *Hale*; and if you would have the Faith to trust him with your Purse and your Person, he will have the Assurance to practice thereon at his own Discretion.

The least smatterer in our Laws thinks himself qualified to step from the *Bar* to the *Bench*, and will tell you 'tis only his own Modesty is the Obstacle to his Preferment; that his Qualifications are no ways inferior to those of the best Proficiency, only that a more private Life is his Choice.

The greatest Bungler in Mechanicks would be thought an Artist in his Profession, and commence an Action of *Scandalium Magnatum* against any who shall deny his superior Excellency.

We see this Vanity runs thorugh all degrees and conditions fo People, even the meanest Persons are effected therewith; the very *Shoe Boys* in the Streets aim at excelling in their several Stations, and strive for Superiority in the way of their Professions, equal with Persons of a most affluent Power and Condition.

But all sorts of Pride and Vanity that is the oddest, and perhaps the greatest, which consists in Humility: The *Butcher*, who left his Calling and grew a *'Squire*, has publish'd a Print of himself, with a Calf peeping over his Shoulder, and for what end? why not so much to inform, as to surprize the World, *That so great a Man was once a Calf-carrier*; for were you to tell him of his former Employment, you would soon find the Pride of the *Gentleman* has but improv'd the Rage of the *Butcher*.

There is often great Pride in the contempt of Pride, and I have known more Conceit and Indolence in a plain *primitive*

Coat, than in an embroidered Suit; and I am assured that a great many of my Acquaintance and *Friends* about *Bull-and-Mouth-Street*, can bear me out in this great Truth.

Notwithstanding that Gentlemen of the SWORD are my very great Favourites, yet the foolish and inconsiderate of that Profession, are subject, as much as others, to my Contempt and Censure. As I was some time ago taking the Air in *Hide-Park*, I saw at a Distance, a young Figure in a Military Garb, his Hat, Cue, and Cockade seem'd ready pinch'd for Execution; his Sword Hilt up to his Elbow, and his distant Air look'd very smart and Soldierly; but I was surpriz'd on a nearer View to see him stagger in his Gate, his Knees contending with every little Breeze, and his Wire-drawn Legs hardly able to support him; by a black Patch on his Nose, and a flannel Bandage round his Neck, I soon guess'd the unhappy Creature's Condition: I discovered he was an Ensign of the Guards, and had the blasted Appearance of something considerable; yet, I own, his Wretchedness could not move my Compassion, that a Man should waste those Limbs in Debauchery, which he hired out for the Service of his Country, is as much a Publick Injustice, as it is a private Misfortune. Every Soldier is a Servant to the State, paid and maintain'd in that Capacity; and is neither to be pitied nor excused when at any Time he disables himself from doing his Duty: And whatever his pretended Bravery may be, he must cease to be an Heroe that is dwindling away by a filthy Distemper. I utterly exclude all those tottering Prodigals from my Favour; for I can neither defend them among the standing Forces, nor can I pity them as broken Officers.

How fickle is the Humour of this World! since *Michaelmas* Lamps have been lighted, I have not heard one Sigh at the Fall of *Opera*'s. The two *Segniora*'s that some time ago were considerable enough to run us into Parties, and to create

Debates about their respective Excellencies, are not gone off unlamented, hardly spoken of; for my own Part, I retain'd the Gentility of my *Goust* to the very last, and with great Concern bid adieu to my dear *Cuzzoni*. She and her Company left in my Charge the following Properties to be disposed of, that the good People of *England* might have more than Songs for their Money.

An INVENTORY of GOODS to be seen near the *Opera-House* in the *Hay-Market.*

For SALE, by Inch of Candle, near the Opera-House *in the* Hay-Market.

A Rising-Sun, second-hand, eclips'd five Digits by the dirty Hands of an Opera-Porter.

A Full Moon, span new, never used, but one Side a little Rat-eaten.

Several Sets of Clouds, flying down the Wind, in good Condition.

Six Dozen of pretty twinkling Stars, a little out of Order for want of brushing.

Four Mantles of State, made in the Reign of King CHARLES II. And worn by Emperors of several Ages and Nations: They are rich Embroidery, and still very fit for Kettle-Drum Banners, or to make Petticoats for running Footmen.

Four dozen of Musick-Books, with long Symphonies and Ha-ha's, very proper Pills for Asthmatick People.

All the Pikes, Javelins, and Partizans of *Alexander*'s Life-Guard, may not serve the Train-Band Officers, either to fight, or to make into Fishing Rods.

Four Brocade Breeches, worn by *Nicolini* and *Senefino*, cut into upper Leathers for Ladies Slippers; the Wastebands bespoke to line the Cape of Mother *Needham*'s Cloak.

Three dozen of *Roman* Sandals and Buskins, made by the best Hand in Cambro-Alley, of the antique Fashions, and very well suited to the modern Taste.

Several other Rarities that we want *English* Names for, but are very useful to the Curious, — and are to be exposed at the Place of SALE.

Among all the Vices, Follies, and Extravagancies of the Age, I am surprised at the present luxurious and fantastical manner of Eating, which many of our People of Quality and false Taste are fallen into. Magnificence and Hospitality are certainly highly commendable in Persons of large Fortunes, but can any Folly be greater than that of laying out as much upon a single Plate to please the affected Palate of one of these foppish Gluttons, as would in Days of ancient Hospitality, have half seated in a Parish? That is, when the old Nobility and Gentry of *England* thought it a greater Honour to have the Praises of their Tenants and the Prayers of the Poor, than the Credit of being able to devour at one selfish Meal what would support a moderate Family in a Twelvemonth.

I question if *Apicius*, mentioned by *Juvenal*, as the greatest of all Gluttons, and who wrote a Book of Instructions how to move Appetite, were he now upon the Stage, would not be rank'd among the Mechanicks in Eating, compared with some of our modern *Epicures*.

I was the other Day at a Person of Quality's House near *Hanover-Square*, who has the Vanity to give forty Pounds a Year to a *French* Man Cook to spoil all the Meat that comes to his Table. I had been there ten Days, and in all the Time could never tell what the Name of any one Thing was that I had eaten, they were all so dignified with Rgou's, forc'd Meats, &c. At last, going one Day accidentally into the Kitchen, I was most agreeably surprised to see half a Dozen Partridges roasting at the Fire, when all on a sudden the Rascally Cook whips them off the Spit and began to pound them in a Mortar, with all the Fat and the Inside of a Surloin of Beef; I ask'd him the Reason of this strange Havock, and he told me, it was to make a *Cullis* for a *Pupton.*

It being no small Mortification to me to see two such excellent Dished thus spoiled, and my Stomach being at the same time pretty sharp set, I had a very reasonable Curiosity to enquire whether was to be any other Dish to make amends for the Disappointment of two, which till this Time I always thought were, without any Adulteration, in the first Class of good Eating; upon which this Heathen of a Cook, to continue his Legerdemain both with my Understanding and Appetite still farther, produced his Bill of Fare, which I chuse to present my readers with in the following Order, by way of illustrating what I have said of the Affectation and Folly of this way of Eating.

1ST COURSE.

Soupe de Santè.

Soupe au Bourgoife.

2D COURSE.

Carp au Court Boillon.

Cutlets a la Maine.

BEEF à la Tremblade

Pupton of Partridge

3D COURSE.

Fricafee of Salamanders

Huffle of Chickens

A Stewed Lyon

Pain Perdu

Oysters a là Daube

Blanc Manger

I will venture to affirm, that there is nothing in this extraordinary Bill of Fare that would not have been more pleasing to the Taste, wholesomer, and every way beter, dress'd in a plain manner; nor has it any thing to recommend it but the Expence and hard Names; for you must know, these sort of *Epicures* do not consult so much their Health or their Palate in their Dishes, as they do the Uncommenness of them, for which Reason I knew a Person of great Distinction, upon his being obliged to entertain a foreign Nobleman, after he has consulted all the *French* cooks and all the Books of Cookery in Town, and finding nothing but what he thought too common for his Table upon so an extraordinary Occasion, resolved to fetch his Dinner out of the Hedges and Ditches, and had his first Course served up in the following manner.

> Viper Soup
> Stew'd Snails
> Couple of Roast Hedge Hogs
> Fricafee of Frogs
> Badger's Ham and Colliflowers

I believe no Body will doubt but that this Gentleman had the End he proposed in providing an uncommon Entertainment, for tho' we read in the Scripture of Guests that were bidden to a Marriage Feast out of the Highways, yet I dare say this was the first Feast itself that ever was furnished from thence.

Altho' I have not mentioned a hundredth Part of the Fopperies of this ridiculous Mode, yet I am persuaded the two extraordinary Specimens I have given you, will be sufficient to convince you that instead of lavishing your Wit and Satyr against Innovations in our publick Diversions only, you ought to reserve some Part for the Absurdities that creep into our private Families.

As a glittering Appearance gains a popular Esteem amongst the Vulgar, it is no Wonder to see our vain-glorious Coxcombs so fond of a gaudy Equipage; but to anatomize these Animals, and shew them in their proper Colours, may possibly afford some Diversion; for when a Fool sets up for a Fop he is no more the Subject of a wife Man's Esteem, than a Caterpillar after it is transform'd to a Butterfly.

The Character of a FOP.

HE is the Superficies of a Ma, and the Magazine of Superfluities, and consults his Taylor with as much Care as the ancient *Greeks* did the Oracle at *Delphi*: He has a particular Regard to the Sabbath, especially after he has purchased a new Peruke, and is never so devout as when he prays for fair Weather; yet he is very wavering in his Religion, for he visits half a dozen Churches in Sermon-time, and never tarrieth long in a Place, but where he can hew his Dress to some Advantage: He looks upon Rain and Wind as the greatest Judgments of Heaven, and had rather run against the D—l in a dark Night than a Chimney-Sweeper; for which Reason he passes *Cheapside-Conduit* with the same Precaution as a poor Citizen does *Woodstreet Compter*: His Politicks are upon the same Foot with his Religion, for before Noon he runs his Head into twenty Coffee-Houses, and has no small Ambition to be thought a News-Monger: He is no great Friend to the Tobacconist, for Fear of his Lungs, yet he holds a Pipe in his Mouth to make his Diamond Ring the more conspicuous, and to that End he has an excellent Faculty in playing upon the Table with his Fingers: He is very careful in adjusting his Phiz, and takes a Pinch of Snuff with the utmost Curiosity; and, at the same Time, reckons him an unmannerly Clown that will not praise his Snuff-Box: His Habiliments are mostly Foreign, and nothing is admirable but what is done by an outlandish Artificer; the Blade of his Sword was temper'd at *Toledo*, and the Handle was wrought by the best Workman in *Andalusia*; nay, the very Head of his Cane was dug out of a Mine in the *Pharsalian* Fields, and afterwards polished by an *Æthiopian* in *Prester John*'s Country. If his Patrimony will allow him a Footman, the poor Fellow is hurried off his Legs with carying *Billet Doux* to the Ladies, and often gets his Head broke for his Master's Impertinence; however, he gets a Smatch of his Master's Airs, and is initiated in the Price of Powder, Essence, Snuff and Washballs: If the Fop keeps a Mistress, according to Fashion, his Pride is too great to be over-courteous; so she must never expect him to dispence his Favour in the Day-time, for a true Fop will starve a thousand other Sins to support his Vanity; and by Consequence he had rather be gelt than discommode a *Flanders* Lace Chitterling. His Wit is like his Habit, or the newest Fashion; and was it Treason to adulterate our Language, as it is to counterfeit the Coin, he would stand a notable Change to be guarded up *Holbourn-Hill* by the Sheriff's Officers; for he affects unintelligible Terms of Speech, and, like an Apothecary, will reduce a whole Sentence into a Monosyllable; yet, if a Man of Honour will afford him a Smile, he is not so concise in his Compliments, but displays himself in a Compound of *French, Indian*, and broken *Latin*, to adorn his Peacock's Feathers with a little Pedantry. If he hears a second-hand Saying at the Coffee-house, he immediately takes the Minutes down in Short-hand; for having but little Brains in his Head he has a natural Tendency to Forgetfulness, and nothing less than a new invented Oath will make a lasting Impression upon his Mind, without the Use of his Common-place Book. He goes to the Play like a true Critick, and pretends to distinguish what is genuine and what is sophisticated; and to prove himself one of a penetrating Judgment he'll curse the Actors, and damn the whole Performance; nay the celebrated *Wilks* and *Booth* cannot escape his Censure, though all the time his Eyes are upon the Ladies, and his Thoughts lifted up that some of them *per* Chance, may be smitten with his fine Appearance. Thus the simple Animal is composed of Pride, Ignorance, Conceit, Vain-glory and Imagination, and Men of Sense withdraw from him as from a pestilential Infection; and indeed nothing can give a prodigal Fop more Mortification than to take no Notice of him, for he knows no other End of his Being than to swagger in the Streets, and resort to publick Places to be gaz'd at; for which Reason he is the only Person that rejoiceth at *Adam's* Fall, otherwise he must have gone naked; and his Soul is too narrow to take a View of Things beyond Brutality: His greatest Enemy is Poverty; and Death itself is not so formidable as a Coat that is wore Thread-bare: Thus if Misfortunes once attack him, the Burden is insupportable, and the last Extremity is to steal a Rope to hang himself. Thus a supercilious Life brings an ignominious Death, and for want of Reason to guide his Passions, Sir Foppington falls into Despair, and dies in Suicide.

Last Summer I happen'd to be at *Bristol*, and coming up in the Stage-Coach I was agreeably diverted with a Narrative that is well worth Notice. There was in Company a grave Merchant, and ancient Gentlewoman, a young *Irishman*, two young Ladies, and myself; the Merchant said little, the old Gentlewoman heard little, the Beaux and the two Ladies had all the Discourse, and I sat as Judge to determine the Controversy. The Theme was *Love*, which argued and defended with a great deal of Judgment on both Sides. The first Night on the Road he took me aside and told me, he believ'd them to be good Natur'd Ladies, for that they had

granted him an Appointment, and that he doubted not but
e'er Morning to gain the Ascendant over them; and accordingly next Day affirm'd to me, he had been happy in their
Embraces. This he confirm'd with such circumstantial Prob-
abilities, that I readily believ'd it Matter of Fact. But how
was he struck with Shame and Confusion, when he found
the two young Ladies metamorphos'd into two young Gentlemen, that for their Diversion, and to pass the Time away,
had purposely put on the Disguise to conceal their Sex, and
had assum'd an Air suitable to their Appearance, to mortify
some fond, conceited, passionate and whining Enamorado.

It may seem romantic, but it is very true that there are
a sort of People who take Pains to be IDLE; such are your
Hunters of News and *Hunters of Levees*, who tramp it half a
Score Streets to know who has got a Wife or a Place.

The *Hunters of Levees* are recorded for three Hours Patience and Attendance with a *gracious Grin*, and come away
well contented; and your Superficial *Visitants*, who go to see
Folks because they are not at Home. There are several others
of this kind, who as it were, *labour to be Lazy.*

It must be owned in the Defence of IDLENESS, that there
are some publick Advantages arising from it, and that it pro-
digiously advances the Exise, by filling of Coffee-Houses,
Tipling-Houses and Taverns. An honest Fellow gets Drunk,
because he has nothing else to do; and a Coffee-House Orator
gives his Jaws *a Breathing*, because he has no *other* Work upon
his Hands. And by the Idleness of our Nobility, Gentry and
Tradesmen, Hackney-Coachmen, Hackney-Harlots, Gamesters, Pimps and Chairmen are supported.

How natural is it to be doing somewhat! Some or other of
our Organs are perpetually craving for Employment: Hence
it is, that a Coquet shivers when she is not Cold, and a Beau

cries *Damn me*, tho' he knows that such a Prayer is altogether superfluous, and tucks down his Ruffles, tho' before they were as smooth as a Lawyer's Tongue.

The common Methods of wearing away our Days, are as various as the Humours and Capacities of Manking. Some lead Armies, some disturb the Publick in a *civil Way*. Some make Speeches, and some pick their Teeth. Snuff has great and universal Reputation this Way, and the Takers of it can recreate their whole Body with a little Labour of the Fingers and the Nose. I know an eminent Sergeant at Law, who finds curious Diversion in drawing a String through his Fingers, and tying Knots upon it; and most of his *learned Brethren* keep themselves in Practice, by stroaking down the sides of their Perriwigs, with remarkable Gravity. The Ladies divert themselves with Tea and Slander, and Visits and their Fans, and several other Amusements, about which I shall say nothing. There are some *few* of both Sexes, who find Devotion as good a Strategem as any, to shake off Time, and so make Piety a considerable Diversion. With others Gaming is in great Repute, for wasting their Money and their Time with wonderful Facility. About the *Royal-Exchange*, Tricking and Over-reaching are notable and approved Cures for Laziness; but at Court they are by no means known or practiced.

I am almost of Opinion, that the Use of Speech, does no great Honour to that Man, who talks only to shew that he talks Nonsense; and yet this is the Case and the Fate of many more accomplished Persons. A Beau, if he would hold his tongue, might hide his *inward Nakedness*; but while he Prates and shews his Teeth, tho' we are convinced that his Mouth or rather his Gums, are well inhabited, we are at the same time let into a Discovery that his Head is a dark and unfurnished Garret. I should be glad I could for *their* Sakes, persuade sev-

eral hopeful young Gentlemen of my Acquaintance, who are
distemper'd with an Opinion of their own Parts, to grow Cunning and hold their Tongue. I wish this Advice of mine be
not *above their Capacity*, I am sure it is for their Interest, and
would they take it, I am almost confident it would be a Secret
to many of those who *only see them*, that they are so entirely
destitute of Reason and most other Gifts which came of God.
I have great Compassion upon our Coffee-House Orators, and
those who at publick Ordinaries daily strain their Throats for
the Interest of *Christendom*, and judiciously distribute their
deep Ignorance and Conjectures, to such as sit round them,
and have the Courtesy to bear Witness *that they are Ideots.*
It would be great Wisdom in the Fools of this Town, if they
would learn the Sense to smother their Nonsense, and then
it would be a great Comfort to all who come within Ear Shot
of them. As for me, I have brought my self to be easy in the
midst of Noise and Absurdity, by a Method which I would recommend to every Body. When a simple Son begins to scatter
Words, all the Notice I take is, that his Mouth is merry and
dancing a Horn-pipe to the Tabor of his Throat; and I cannot
but think, an honest foolish Fellow may lawfully play with his
own Chaps as well as with his Legs or his Cane. I have carried
my Humour further in this Case: With me, every Man who
talks falsely or foolishly, does not talk at all: No, I am resolved
that the dishonest Speaker and the ridiculous Prater, are, and
shall be dumb Men; and I wish for the peace and Ease of the
World, that all Mankind were of my Opinion: A braying Booby would not then disturb us, not a knavish Orator mislead
us. I am so delighted with this philosophical Artifice of mine,
that I often go to *see* a Man speak on purpose not to *hear* him;
it is therefore no Wonder that I have in my Time beheld both
Lawyers and Divines eloquently dumb for an Hour or two to-

gether: I have found most pretenders to Physick more *copious* and *silent* than any other sort of Men, and no People in this Town are so vehemently and so learnedly *Mutes* as Politicians and Cricks. — The first that calls a Man a Fool is himself, and others do but take it from his own Mouth. When a weak Person shuns a Discovery *by keeping his Tongue within his Teeth* as the Proverb has it, we generally assign a kind Cause for his Silence, and believe it to be the Effect of good Sense, which is never very forward; but if his Tongue betrays him, and shews him a *Soft-head*, the World is not to blame for passing *Sentence*, when he himself has confessed the *Guilt*.

The late proceedings in our Courts of Law have furnished us with ample Proofs, that this Town abounds too plentifully with a Sect of brutish Creatures called SODOMITES; a Sect that ought to be excluded from all civil Society and human conversation. They exceed the worst Beasts of the Field in the Filthiness of their Abominations The Birds of the Air couple Male and Female to propagate Generation, and every Animal moved by a natural Instinct; but Man, exclusive of all others, forms Ideas destructive to himself, and grows fond of new Inventions which are repugnant to divine Institution and the fundamental Laws of Nature; he is grown hardened in Inquity, having abandon'd himself to all manner of Vice, and is not ashamed to act Crimes which expose him to the Severity of the Laws and the Contempt of the World. I have heard that one *Tolson*, who lately kept a Brandy-Shop at *Charing-Cross*, and was transported for Felony, whose Constitution was so depraved and ruined that he could contain nothing within him, and who was not ashamed to confess, that he received that Debility by human Conversation and the vile Practice of Buggery; and that once having caught a Foot-Soldier in Bed with his Wife, he insisted upon no other Satisfaction than to commit the detestable Sin of Sodomy with him, which the other comply'd with, and so the Affair was made easy. It is a melancholy Sight to see Men in full Strength and Vigour go to publick Executions unpitied and unlamented, loaded with the highest Guilt, that can neither hope or expect any Mercy in this, and may justly dread the Punishments in the World to come: The greatest Criminal has some People that may drop some pitying Expressions for his unhappy and untimely Fate and condole his dismal Circumstances; while those Persons who fall by the Laws for *Sodomy*, can expect neither Pity or Compassion. It would be a pretty Scene to behold them in their Clubs and Cabals, how they assume the Air and affect the Name of *Madam* or *Miss*, *Betty* or *Molly*, with a chuck under the Chin, and *O you bold Pullet I'll break your Eggs*, and then frisk and walk away to make room for another, who thus accosts the affected Lady, with *Where have you been you fancy saucy Queen? If I catch you Strouling and Caterwauling, I'll beat the Milk out of your Breasts I will so*; with a great many other Expressions of Buffoonry and ridiculous Affectation. If they can procure a young smug-fac'd Fellow they never grudge any Expence, and it is remarkable these effeminate Villians are much fonder of a new *Convert* than a Bully would be of a new *Mistress*.

They have also their *Walks* and *Appointments*, to meet and pick up one another, and their particular Houses of Resort to go to, because they dare not trust themselves in an open Tavern. About twenty of these sort of Houses have been discovered, besides the nocturnal Assmblies of great Numbers of the like vile Persons, what they call the *Markets*, which are the *Royal-Exchange, Lincolns-Inn Bog-Houses*, the South-side of St. *James's Park,* the Piazzas of *Convent-Garden*, St. *Clement's Church-Yard,* &c.

The Town is now come to that Height of Wickedness, that every parish might now employ five or six Satyrists, besides as many Parsons; not that I think the latter so remiss in their Duty as to need the Assistance of the Press, but the capricious Humours of the People make it as necessary as it is to have an Adjutant in a Regiment as well as a Colonel, that where the Courtesy of a Man will not prevail, a King *Harr*'s Knock may do it more effectually.

Should our Priests speak to the People as they did in Days of Yore, they would become the Ridicule of every Scoundrel; for now nothing will pass for good Sense, but St. *Gregory*, St. *Austin*, St. *Athanasius*, &c. and if there comes not a little *Latin*, or *Greek*, and sometimes *Hebrew* too into the Bargain, it goes down no better than a Joint of Veal without Sauce: Whereas, did not the Prejudice of Custom deprive us of plain Truth, and down-right Honesty, the Priest might (without the Imputation of being vulgar) call out, A hah, you Mr. ———, with the black Wig and plush Coat, how dare you keep a Rendezvous for Gaming, drinking, and Whoring? How dare you come to Church before you clear your Conscience? And with no more Remorse than you come from the Tap before you fill the Tankard? Believe me, Sir, if you abandon yourself to these Enormities, and live not up to the Precepts of the Gospel, you'll receive your Reward in a Place that smells as strong of Brimstone as a Bundle of Card-Matches. Now, I say, should he express himself after this Manner, he would appear like the Father of his Flock, and consequently like a Christian; but alas! this wou'd never gain him the Approbation of his Auditory; they would rather look on him as they did on down-right *Daniel Burgess*, of merry Memory, who was the only Man in the Three Kingdoms for a judicious Comparison: *I tell ye*, says *Daniel, Mens Hearts are like Womens Smocks, fine at Top, but coarse at Bottom*; at which the wild Part of the People burst into a Laughter, so that the poor Man was oblig'd to give them this *Salvo* for their private Satisfaction, viz. *That he did not know it by Experience, but by seeing 'em hang on the Hedges.* Now, Sit, 'tis under this Consideration that I would have the Poets exert their Authority; for till we banter the Town from their most capital Vices, they will never give Heed to *General Heads*, no not so much as to the Head of an Onion, for that indeed will make them weep if they have an Heart of Adamant. But alas! ten *general Heads*, with Doctrine, Use and Application to attend them, are not received with half the Alacrity as a *single Ten of Diamonds.*

   I live in a Parish, which to its Honour, be it spoken, is one of the largest and most populous in the Bills of Mortality, yet a Man might wear out a pair of the best Shoes in Christendom in it, before he finds a Person truly virtuous, except it be my self, and two or three of my Acquaintance, together with Mr. *h*——*S* the Talley-Man. — But hold, I forgot Mr. *s*—*D* the Attorney, and old *n*——*A* the predestinated Pawn-broker: Now, I say, Sirs, is it not a Shame, a burning Shame, for a Man to think on, that I who have liv'd sixteen Years in a Parish, yet cannot find above six Persons in it that are just in their Morals, charitable to the Poor, and sincere in their Devotion: But what makes the Wickedness of the Wicked more aggravating is, that these pious Men cannot escape the Imputation of being as bad as their Neighbours, tho' good Christians are of another Opinion, and I heard a Man of Fourscore declare it, he believed they could not match them for their Exactness in Dealing, and singular Conversation, from *Mile-End* to *Mill-Bank* at *Westminster*.

   Nothing weakens the Mind and turns the Brain more than the delusive Horrors which the common Stories of

Dæmons and *Goblings* bring along with them. He that is the staunchest Believer in this Point, is often the most wretched Infidel in Articles of the highest and most useful Nature. He swallows glibly the grossest Falsehoods and Forgeries, but cannot bear the Acceptance of Truth and Conviction. If you tell him that a *Spirit* carried away the Side of a House, or play'd at Foot-ball with half a dozen Chairs and as many Pewter-dishes, you win his Heart and Assent; but if you go about to persuade him that a bodily Communication between the *invisible Spirits* of the other World and the mortal Inhabitants of this, is not very likely, at least not very common, he holds up both his Hands and wonders how you can be so great an Atheist. Such a one is so long accustomed to be cheated by others and himself, that at length nothing but Delusion will go down with him, and he has no Relish for what is not Monstrous and opposite to Nature and Probability.

In the Country there are two Sorts of *Ghosts*, a *Plebian Ghost* and a *Ghost of Rank*; and these two bear a different Figure, and have a different Behaviour.

The Ghost of Dignity is always known to be the Spirit of a former Landlord of the Parish, who visits his Tenants every Night in a Coach and Six, and rattles round his Mansion-House, to see that nothing be amiss, and to frighten the Servants in to their Duty. His *Ghost* is the very same Man that he himself was in his Life-time, in every Respect: It wears the self-same Snuff-colour'd Cloaths trimm'd with black, the same Camblet-Cloak, lin'd with red, a little faded, and the same Shoes with Cork-Soals and square-Toes. Its Gloves are lin'd with Lambskin, and it has Fustain Drawers on, just as the 'Squire had. Nay, the Spirit has upon its Body all the Marks that had been upon the Body of the 'Squire; the little Wart under the left Ear, the small Scar upon the little Finger, the Dimple in the Chin, and twenty other Signs and Tokens, which are all visible to any Man, Woman, or Child, that can but see clearly in the Dark.

Farthermore, our *Ghost* has the Ways and Humours which it had when it was alive. It Smiles upon one Servant, casts a Frown at another, and loves Noise and stale Beer, as well as when it followed a Pack of Hounds all Day, and sate up with another Pack all Night: For great Hooping and hollowing are often heard in the Parlour of the Cellar about Two in the Morning, and, upon Examination, a Barrel of *October* is found empty. Well fare his Worshipful Heart; it is not the first of a Thousand, that he has serv'd in the same Manner.

Sometiems his Worship is sadly out of Temper, and more outrageous than a reasonable dead Man should be; but he has good Cause for it. — His extravagant Son and Heir, has, perhaps, lost Three and Six-pence at Whisk, or bought a glander'd Horse, or sold his Sheep and his Barley too cheap, or done some such important and unfrugal Fault. This is Provocation enough in Conscience for the grey-headed old *Ghost*, who remembers what bodily Pains it took to get Riches, to fret and stamp, and throw down all the Pewter Dishes about the House. And yet I cannot see why his late Worship should pinch the innocent Children for their Father's Errors; or why he should terrify the Kennel of Dogs, as often as he does, and set them a howling, as if the poor Beagles were his Son's Counsellors, when, in Truth, they are only his *Principal Companions*.

It happens, sometimes, that the departed *old Gentleman* is seen and heard weeping and wailing most bitterly over a Pong in the Garden, and then it is a hundred to one but a Child or a Coach-Horse dies some time or other afterwards. I own, indeed, that the *Ghost* does not alone possess, in his own single

Person, this kind of *foretelling Spirits*; for the *old House-Dog* is likewise a Prophet of this King, and never howls, but something or other comes after it; and the *Crickets* in the Wall have an admirable Knack at *fore-smelling a Funeral.*

These *Ghosts of Quality* have, in their Way of *living*, one Circumstance which I would not forget. The cunning Creatures, when they are *dead*, and *gone*, and *rotten*, have Policy enough to return to their own Houses, and to take up the best Rooms there for themselves to lodge in. And if any Man presume to lye in their Beds, they never fail to kick him, and cuff him, and toss him in a Blanket. So unsociable and malicious do People grow when once they are lock'd up in their Coffins. *This shews that dead Folks can bite.*

Having now done due Honour to *Ghosts of Fashion*, I go on to say something about *vulgar Apparitions*; and there is this essential Difference between them; *a Spirit of Title and Figure is ever more formidable and mischievous than a Spirit of low Fortune, or meanly born.* So that we see the Temper of Men is the same in both Worlds.

A poor Ghost does not constantly appear in its own bodily Likeness, but humbly contents it self with the Body of a *white Horse*, that gallops about the Meadows without Legs, and grazes in them without a Head. On other Occasions it wears the Carcass of a *great black Dog*, that glares full in your Face, but neither bites you, nor says an uncivil Word to you. Sometimes it gives *three solemn Raps* at your Door, and if you do not answer it, it says nothing to you; and if you do answer it, it holds its Tongue.

There are several other Marks and Particularities belonging to *humble Plebeian Ghosts*, as their leaving their Footsteps in the Ashes, their taking you by the Hand when you are asleep, and the like. But the chief Affair that calls them back

again to *visit the World by Night*, is their Fondness for a Pot of
Money which they buried in their Life-time, and cannot be at
Rest in their Graves without it. Thus the thirst of Gold raises
them before the Resurrection.

GET MONEY, said a wiser Man than you or I, honest
Reader: That is the Precept, but he went no farther, leaving
the Business of Committee-Men, Ways and Means, to the peculiar turn of Thought of Bias of Invention or every individual
Money-Getter.

Of all the Methods made use of to attain this great End,
I believe it will be allow'd, that he who gains this Point the
easiest way is the wisest Person: For instance, I know there are
Gold and *Silver* Mines in *Peru* and *Mexico*, but then I consider,
it is at a very inconvenient Distance, and a thousand Toils
and Dangers must be undergone, before we can have a chance
to pocket a single Ingot of either. What is to be done in this
Case? we can't go to them, and they will not come to us. In this
Plunge of Affairs we have seen some late notable Instances of
the Dexterity of our Countrymen for removing the abovesaid
Difficulties: Say they, *Let the* Spaniards *and* Portugese *sail to
the* Indies, *the* Dutch, French, *and* English, *to all the other Parts
of the World, and we will snack in their Treasure, without stiring
them from this wicked Spot of the Earth the Town.*

The late famous SHEPARD, of Housebreaking memory, de-
clared (it seems) at the Gallows, that he had laid a Foundation
for raising the Reputation of the *British Thievery* to a greater
Height than it's been carried in the preceeding Ages: And if
the Relations we see daily published can be depended on, it
may justly be said, we have lived to see his Words verified.
But perhaps some will think that I am wandering beyond my
Province when I am going to prove, that Filching is as old as
the World; that it has been the Practice of all Ages and Na-

tions; that the greatest of Men have endeavour'd to keep it in Countenance: And in a word, I think I can prove, that all Men are Thieves, tho' very few have the honesty to confess it. The first Theft was committed in Paradise, and the first Thief was our universal Mother, to the Honour of the fair Sex be it spoken; who, influenced by so good an Example, have to this Day kept up their laudable Appetite for pilfering; as appears by the numerous Complaints you hear of doleful Swains, whose Hearts have been purloin'd. In this I think they have got the start of us; we can prove our first Sire no more than a Receiver at best; and the Proverb will not allow the Receiver to be as good as the Thief. After this no body will controvert the Antiquity of this Art.

It remains then, that something be said for the Honour of our own Sex; who, tho' they cannot boast of being the Inventors of it, yet I hope to shew, that they have made as many Improvements on it, and carried it to as high a pitch as it would bear. The *Jews* stealing every thing they could wrap and rend it from the *Ægyptians* at their Departure, is an exploit that we shall come, in for at least half the Glory of, tho' it should be allowed, that the Ladies (as it often happens in modern Marches) carried the Knapsacks, and the Men only bore their Arms. He must be very ignorant of History; who knows not, that the *Ægyptians*, a learned and wise Nation, held this Art in such high Esteem, that they severely punish'd ignorant Pretenders to it. Antient Writers assure us, that a Theft cleverly perform'd, intituled the Artist to the Booty purloined; but if he was so aukward, as to be detected before the Completion of his purpose, he was turn'd over to the Hands of old *Father Antique*, the *Law*. The *Lacedemonians* were so well appriz'd of the great Use and Advantage of this Art, that they early instructed their Children in the commendable Practice of Filching; and

every one knows, that the *Lacedemonians* were always reputed
a wise and famous People; tho' it be certain, that no other of
the polite Arts and Sciences got footing amongst them. So remarkable an Instance as that of *Romulus* must not be omitted:
He very wisely raked together a parcel of Thieves; and they became the Progenitors of a Set of People, who, while they kept
up to the Virtues of their Ancestors, were the most powerful,
the most learned, and the most polite Nation in the World;
but when they grew rich, and their Opulence set them above
practicing those *Virtues*, they dwindled into nothing.

That it has been the universal Practice (and often the only
Knowledge) of all Philosophers, will be evident, upon a comparison of their several Notions and Systems. I would avoid
an Ostentation of Learning in this Place, or I could make my
Reader stare at my profound Sagacity in discussing the Tenets,
and discovering the Thefts of the Antients one from another:
But familiar Examples will be more suitable to the Genius and
Capacity of several of my courteous Readers: And therefore I
will content my self with putting them in mind of the late horrible Robberies attempted upon Mr. G—B---N, Mr. ED—DS,
&c. and of an Expression made use of by the renowned *Roger
John—n*, upon two of the Persons concern'd in them on their
being brought to *Newgate*; viz. *That had he their Opportunities
and Advantaged joined to his Head, he would not have left the
Bank of* England *worth a Groat in half a Year's time.*

As there is nothing more *Lawless* than the *Passions*, when
they are left to themselves, what a miserable *Slave* must that
Person be, who gives himself up to their *Dominion*: All he
studies is present Gratification, let the Consequence be what
it will, the *Gallows* or *Damnation*. One *Libertine*, for the Enjoyment of a beastly Strumpet, poison'd with Quicksilver and
the Pox, slings away his Health and risques his Soul, kills or

rather murders his Innocent Wife, and most paternally entails *Rottenness* and an *infamous Example* upon his Posterity. *Another* mad with Wine and *Wrath* runs his Sword into a poor Man's Heart, and sends him into another World, *with all his Sins upon his Head*; and perhaps at the same time makes Beggars of a *Widow* and a House full of *Children*, who all depended upon *that one Life*. A *third* is under the absolute Government of Pride or Ambition, and ruins his Fortune and his Family by Expence and Equipage; and makes himself Little by striving to be Great, and Poor by endeavouring to be Rich.

Tim. Turbulent, is a Practitioner of vast Business in the Law: He is continually writing Letters and sending Porters to himself. If in Termtime you meet him in the Streets, he can scarce spare time to bend his Head at you; and if his Mouth opens you are sure to be deafen'd with a Noise about *Declarations, Counsel, Costs*, and the like: But for all this Bustle and Industry, *Tim* was never known to have brought a Cause to Issue in his Life-time, excepting formerly, one in the *Marshal*'s Court, in which himself was the *Defendant*.

Ned Needy, was never worth five Pounds during the whole Course of his Life, and has been often hard put to it, to procure Credit for a Week's Lodging, or a clean Shirt. *Ned* never fails in all conversation to boast of the happy Situation of his Affairs, and the vast Affluence and Reputation he exists in. *Nick Niggard* is on the other hand universally known to be what the World calls a *Plumb Man*: He is for ever complaining of the *hard Times*, and his Poverty; and when he is told of his Wealth, shakes his Head with a Sneer, wishing the Suggestion could be made good, *&c.* Thus the one, who is possess'd of a real Substance, is as industrious in concealing it, as the other, who had none at all, is, in endeavouring to make the World believe he has one.

Caleb Kettle, has a Front of the *Corinthian* Order, when he is Master of a Shilling, and as keen as a *Hugonot* just landed from *France*, or a *Welch* Drover, is apt to pop in at the *Pine-apple* or the *Chop-House*: *Caleb* after surveying the Place and the Company, is sure to acquaint them, that he hath not only neglected a plentiful Dinner at home, but his Promise of Dining with some Duke or other great Personage, but that Business, and a Desire withal of Variety, and viewing the Humours of low Life, has drawn him thither. *Kettle*'s a merry destitute Mortal, and has scarce ever fail'd of Dining upon *Constitution-Hill*, or in some *Cook*'s Brothel, every *Christmas-Day* for these twenty Years.

I pity *Beau Bobbish*, he cannot withal the Merit of his lac'd Coat, meet with the least Reverence from any of his Fellow Creatures, except his *Japanner*, and the *Porter* that pimps for him, and is his Confident and Letter Carrier. He therefore picks his Teeth all the Afternoon at *Dicks*, where every Quarter of an Hour he is sending for the said Porter, his Plenipotentiary, on Purpose to be ravish'd with those two pretty Words, *Your Honour*.

Tom Terrible ridicules the Notion of a Deity in all company he comes into; and *D—ns his Blood* with a Bon Grace five hundred times a Day; and would fain pass for a polite and fashionable Atheist, which seems to be at the Height of his Ambition; though his Mother and the Maid, who light him to Bed, are ready on Oath to attest that *Tom* is the most timerous Animal breathing in his Quarters; that he has more than fifty times disturbed the Family in the Night time, with his Apprehensions of seeing *Spirits*. Nay, they go farther, and say he never ventures to Bed without his Prayers.

A most surprising Spirit of NOVELTY has newly discover'd itself in the Town, proceeding, it seems, from a few Bankrupt

Tradesmen, undone some by Negligence, and some by Misfortune, who having contracted an idle and loitering Habit of Life, and made shirt by Remnants of Composition Money to pop themselves behind the Bars of Coffee-Houses, have all on a sudden determin'd to turn Regulators, Authors, Eves-droppers, News-Writers, Committee-Men, Orators, and what not; and having proclaim'd in publick Print, *That their Houses are the Grand Magazines of Intelligence*, have had the Confidence to publish Two Papers with such *Portions of Foreign and Domestick News, that I believe never before appear'd in Print in this or any other Nation.* These Gentlemen having set out with great Ambition, and met with humble Success, I shall endeavor to rescue their *Daily-Labours* from that State of Obscurity they may have hitherto lain under by *publishing* them to the World, *viz.*

Hounslow, Jan. 23.

'Fifty Batallions, and as many Squadroms, pass'd thro' this City Yesterday, in order to form a Camp upon the Banks of our River, which, with the Troops from *Staynes, Egham,* and the neighbouring Provinces, will make an Army of 35000 Men, which will be abundantly sufficient to prevent any Surprize on that Side of the Country.

Hammersmity, January 25. N.S.

Our Minister here observes so profound a Silence, that no Body hath as yet been able to penetrate into his Designs; notwithstanding, 'tis whisper'd, that he is carrying on a secret Negotiation with the Court of *Chelsea.*

Lambeth, January 30.

A Master of a Ship, who arriv'd here in One and Twenty Days from *Chelsea*, reports, that the Troops and Pensioners of that Province have Orders to hold themselves in Readiness upon any Emergency, but as they are commanded only to furnish themselves with *Squirts* and *Pot-guns*, 'tis not likely that they are under any great Apprehension.

Brentford, Feb. 1. O.S.

Expresses are continually going to and fro in this City: and 'tis said, that there is great Likelyhood that a Congress will be form'd at *Windsor* by the latter End of next *Summer*.

Wandsworth, Feb. 2.

A Squadron of Men of War has been seen off of this Place, which is suppos'd to be Part of the Fleet which is to join the Admiral of *Mortlake*.

Chiswick, Feb. 3.

Our Country enjoys a perfect Tranquility, and there seems to be that Harmony between our Ministers and those of all the Foreign Courts, that 'tis highly probable we shall have NO SHARE in their Differences.

LONDON

Yesterday great Numbers of People pass'd and repass'd thro' *Fleet-Street, St. Paul's Church-Yard, Cheapside*, and other of the principal Streets of this City, as usual.

The same Day a Dray passing thro' *Chancery-Lane* with several Barrels of Strong Beer on it, one of them rowl'd over into the Street, by which Misfortune about Three Quarts of the Liquor was unluckily lost.

We hear, that Mr. *James* ———, who was Cook at the *Rose Tavern* without *Temple Bar*, and gave an entire Satisfaction to all the Gentlemen that us'd his Master's House, is gone from thence to the *Devil*.

Yesterday a Hackney-Coach founder'd in the *Strand*, near *Sommerset-House*, but by the timely Assistance of the Neighbourbhood all the Passengers were saved.

We are credibly inform'd, That the famous Mr. *Moore* hath undertaken to destroy the Worms that have been of such pernicious Consequence to our Shipping in the *West-Indies*, by eating into their Bottoms; and that he will set sail some Time in *March* with Two large Ships, laden with his celebrated *Powder* for that Purpose.

On *Sunday* Night last, when the Corpse of *Tom* the *Tubman* came to be interr'd in *Stepney Church-yard*, the Grave that had been prepar'd for his Reception was stolen away, as is suppos'd, by Three Rogues in Sailors Habits, who had been seen lurking thereabouts some Hours before; and we hear, that Yesterday Morning it was taken up in the *Thames* by *John Edes* the Waterman, who took up the great overgrown Owl that was shot on the Top of the *York-Buildings* Water-house, as mention'd in one of our former. Some Days since an odd sort of an Accident happen'd near *Blackwall*, where the Ship *Sarah* and *Johanna* from *Lisbon*, lades with Lemons and Oranges, the *Judith* from *Nantz* with Brandies, and the *Lucy* from *Jamaica* with Sugars, falling foul of each other with uncommon Violence, were all stav'd to pieces, and in an Instant the River run a perfect and well compos'd *Punch* for many Miles together, to the great Comfort and Relief of the Sea-faring Part of his Majesty's Subjects.'

These extraordinary intelligible Gentlemen have furnish'd us with other Accounts of the like Nature; as Churches knock'd down in the Night Time by Villains, and robb'd of their rich Ornaments; Whales have by them been found in Duckling Ponds and Ditches; the Court has been often sent several Miles out of Town, when not one of the Royal Family has been out of the Palace at that Time: Discoveries have been made of unheard of Villages in the County of *Middlesex*, as well as in other Countries; Noblemen and Gentlemen have been sent to Seats of their own that they never heard of, and dined and supp'd with People they never saw, and cast-off Whores have been reconciled to their *Keepers* even so far as to get married to them; People appear'd in *Westminster-Hall* upon Recognizances that had none to answer, and at a Time when none of the Courts were fitting; Persons and Places given them who had been many Years in their Graves; Gentlemen and Tradesmen been dismounted on the Roads, robb'd of Monies and their Buckles stolen from under their Boots, who were quietly in their Beds at the Times mentioned. These are the *Stores of Intelligence in their own Hands, of which they have been the blind Possessors to this Day.* This is *reforming and bringing Publick Intelligence to the highest Perfection.*

After Measures of this Kind had been carried on for Three Weeks and Three Days, *for the common* BENEFIT *and Relief of the Coffee-men of the Cities of* London *and* Westminster, by publishing *Two Papers, of Half a Sheet each, on every Working Day; one in the above-mentioned Portions of Foreign and Domestick News,* the Subscribers had a General Meeting on *Saturday* the 25th Day of *January* at Night, in order to reap the *Profits and Advantages* with which their *Cares and Exactness had been attended*, by way of DIVIDEND, and *to establish the Undertaking on a legal Foundation, and to procure Securities for every one's Property and Share in it.* The Monies being divided, and proper *Instruments in Law* sign'd and seal'd, they next took into Consideration the *untain* and *Transitory* State of the Things of this *Life*, and knowing that *Papers* as well as *Men* are *mortal*, and must soon or late *die*, they therefore order'd the Printing of their *Paper* to be immediately perform'd near *Exeter Exchange* in the *Strand,* to the End the *worshipful* and *worthy* Company of *Upholders* might be at Hand to decently inter it, in Case of such an Accident.

Several Minutes being read, and the Subscribers made aquainted with every other Preparation and Disposition made by the Managers for persevering in this laudable Undertaking, they were desired to declare their Sentiments of the PROCEED-INGS of the Managers; and all of them declaring they were ex-treamly satisfy'd, and very ready to perform what was enjoin'd them in the great Point of receiving this Sort of Intelligence; and their Two ABLE and EXPERIENCE'D COMPILERS declaring they were ready to stand by them to the last Drop of Ink in their Bottles, and the COLLECTORS while they had Heels to their Shooes or Shirts to their Backs, the Meeting broke up, to the satisfaction of every one present.

FINIS

Satan's Harvest Home:
OR THE
PRESENT STATE
OF
WHORECRAFT,
ADULTERY,
FORNICATION,
PROCURING,
PIMPING,
SODOMY,
And the
GAME at FLATTS

(Illustrted by an Authentick and Entertaining Story)
And other SATANIC WORKS, daily propagated in this
good Protestant Kingdom.

Collected from the Memoirs of an intimate Comrade of the
Hon. *Jack S**n**r*; and concern'd with him in many of his
Adventures.

To which is added,
The PETIT MAITRE, a POEM,
By a Lady of Dictingtion.

LONDON:
Printed for the Editor, and sold at the *Change*, St. *Paul's,
Fleet Street,* by Don against St. *Clement's Church;* LEWIS,
Covent Garden; *Exeter Change*, at *Charing Cross*, and in the
Court of Requests; JACKSON, JOLLIFFE, DODSLEY, BRIND-
LEY, STEIDEL, SHROPSHIRE, CHAPPEL, HILDYARD, at *York*;
LEAK, at *Bath*; and at the Snuff Shop in *Cecil Court,* St.
Martin's Lane, 1749.

47

Satan's Harvest Home

When a person unacquainted with the *Town*, passes at Night thro' any of our principal Streets, he is apt to wonder, whence that vast Body of *Courtezans*, which stands ready, on small Purchase, to obey the Laws of Nature, and gratify the Lust of every drunken Rake-hell, can take its Rise.

Where the Devil do all these B——hes, come from? being a common *Fleet-Street* Phrase, and in the Mouth of every Stranger; when each revolving Evening sends them up from *White-Chapel* to *Charing-Cross;* as plenty as Mackrel after Thunder in hot Season.

The Gallants of this Age indeed, are not quite so sturdy as that *Roman Emperor,* who deflower'd ten *Samaritan* Virgins. They destroy, it is true, a great deal of Beauty by only browsing upon the Buds.

Neither is it entirely from a Wantonness of Fancy, or a luxurious Taste of Pleasure, that Men indulge themselves in making this Havock, but chiefly for their own personal Safety. Young girls are so giddy, thoughtless and unexperienc'd, and withal so fond of the Sport at their first setting out, that they seldom escape a Taint, and a man is not safe in being constant: Nay, some Men are afraid of venturing, even after themselves. By this Means, several likely Women, who might do the Town a signal Service, are in a short Time render'd useless: And, by a modest Computation, we are put to the Expence of as many virtuous Women in one Year, as might reasonably serve the Nation fix.

What a deplorable Sight is it, to behold Numbers of little Creatures pil'd up in Heaps upon one another, sleeping in the publick Streets, in the most rigorous Seasons, and some of them whose Heads will hardly reach above the Waistband of a Man's Breeches, found to be quick with Child, and become burdensome to the Parish, whose Hospitable Bulks and Dung-hils have given them Refuge? I have often thought, that the re-moving these Lay-Stalls of Leachery from the Doors of a great Protestant City, might not be a Work altogether unworthy of our reforming Scavengers.

We often read, indeed, of the mighty Atchievements of a certain *Kn——t,* and the Excursions of Midnight *Consta-bles;* their encount'ring of Dragons in Gin-shops, storming enchanted Night-Cellars, and leading Ladies into Captivity. All which are related with wonderful Exactness in the pub-lick News-Papers. But meet these People when you will, you will seldom find in their Custody above a *Flat-Cap* or a *Cin-der-Wench,* who, because their Rags won't pawn for a Dozen of Beer, are made Examples of. She that has the Prudence to whore with Half a Crown in her Pocket, is as sure of a Pro-tection, as a cheating *Director*, and may sin on without any Danger. While the poor needy *Wag-Tail* must be cautious how she kisses, lest she be carried to *Bridewel*, where, instead of being reclaim'd, she is harden'd by her indelible Shame in her miserable State of Wickedness. The only good they have done, is to put an Impost upon Whoring, and made themselves Col-lectors of the Duty; for which Reason, the Price of Venery is greatly enhanc'd, and that within a few Years, which makes it the more practiced; for the Cheapness of a Commodity always throws it out of Fashion, and Things easily purchas'd are seldom minded. It is a right Observation, that Restraint does but whet the Passions, instead of curing them, as we find in the case of most married Men, who like *Sampson's* Foxes, only do more Mischief for having their Tails tied.

The late Colonel *Chart—s* was indeed of Opinion, that when we caught a fine *Sempstress* or *Mantua-Maker*, in the publick streets after Nine at Night, whether *Banbox'd* or *Bundl'd*, it might still be lawful to charge her in Custody of the first *Hackney* Coach, and convey her to the next Bagnio, as a proper and rightful Chattel of the Publick's; but how far Gentleman's Sentiments will be supported by our Statutes, I must leave to the Determination of the Learned.

The Town being over-flock'd with *Harlots*, is entirely owing to those Numbers of *Women-Servants*, incessantly pouring into it from all Corners of the Universe, and those Debaucheries practis'd upon 'em in almost all the Families that entertain them: *Masters, Footmen, Journeymen, Lodgers, Apprentices, &c.* are for ever attempting to corrupt; and a few young Creatures now-a-days are endow'd with a Stock of Virtue sufficient to hold out against all their Attacks; so that a poor Wench, who serves four or five Pounds a Year Wages, shall be liable to go through as much *Drudgery*, as a Livery-Horse, that's lett out to a City Prentice *for a Sunday's* Airing.

I am told, it is the Custom throughout the *West of England,* that when a young Girl is taking her leave of her Friends and Relations to come for *London* and seek her Fortune, while some of them are wishing her *Grace*, and others a *good Place*, and the Carrier is hoisting her up into his Waggon, to give her a swinging Thump on the Br——ch, saying,

> *Now Hussey a Month's Wages or a Month's Warning,*
> *And to Bed your Master every Morning.*

After they have been a little while in Town, and had some Feather-bed Instruction, and are out of Place, and having nothing to support them, they then prostitute their Bodies. Many of them are as restless as a *new Equipage*, running from Place to Place, from Bawdy-House to Service, and from Service to Bawdy-House again; for, if the Matron uses them ill, away their trip to Service, and if their Mistress but gives them a wry Word, whip they are as ready to be gone, *as a reliev'd Guard*, or a *discharg'd Fury*: so that in Effect, they neither make good Whores, good Wives, or good Servants, and this is one of the chief Reasons why our Streets swarm with Strumpets.

What is more common, than to find the Daughters of mean Tradesmen, basking in their Beds at Ten o'Clock in a Summer's Morning, and when call'd on *to rise*, must have good Assurances of the *Tea-Kettle's* being up before them, e'er they'll vouchsafe to begin to rub their Eyes and Posteriors, and put themselves in a way of slipping on a loose Petticoat, Night-Gown and Slippers; by which, and the Addition of a Foul Handkerchief, a Play-Book, and Snuff-box Miss is completely equipt for the Tea Table.

Thus their silly fond Parents, who perhaps are scarce able to give fifty Pounds Portion with them, indulge them from their Infancy in every slothful Habit. Any idle Complaint suffices, to keep a Child a Week from Work or from School. I have seen my Landlady's Daughters romping about the Streets all the Forenoon: *Children*, said I, *why are you not gone to School? O Sir, we ben't well.*

Impudence and Idleness soon gain the Ascendancy over them, and then it is, that a Wench of fourteen, fancies herself as fit for Man, and ripe for Joy, as a Woman of five and twenty: and then also, we behold a strange Paradox; that a Girl, who cou'd never be taught to the Use of her *Needle*, becomes on a sudden a wonderful Proficient in the Art of *stitching*.

I'll appeal to all the *Bona-Roba*'s in the several Chaces, Parks, and Warrens, *North* and *South* of *Covent-Garden*, and ask whether one in twenty can fairly lay her Hand upon her Heart, and affirm, that the Cause of her Ruin was not more owing to the Pride, Negligence, or Indiscretion of those that undertook to pilot her thro' the early Part of Life, than to any evil Inclinations of her own.

I have often been astonish'd, how any Man or Woman could be so great a Stranger to the Knowledge of Life, as to trust a young Daughter or Niece, in a little *Bawdy Vehicle*, a-long with a rampant Rake, able and ready to ravish a whole Boarding-School, to take a Country Jaunt ten or twelve Miles distant, when every Jolt on the Road, not only gives a kind of Titillation, but even the Situation itself affords the most favourable Opportunity, for a Fellow to rob a Girl of all that's dear to her.

What dreadful Execution hath been done by *Play, Masquerade,* and *Opera* Tickets, especially, when in the Hands of skillful *Engineers.* Not to mention Dancing-bouts and other Merry-makings, which seldom prove such innocent Recreations, as some weak and credulous Parents imagine them to be.

When it is consider'd, what a vast Number of Difficulties a pretty young Orphan is to struggle with in this lewd Age, one would rather think her an Object of *Compassion* than *Adoration*, and instead of calling her *divine*, title her most *miserable Creature*: she is not only to encounter with the frequent Importunities and Opportunities of DESIRING *Brothers-in-law, Uncles, Cousins*, and other *Guardians*, in whose Power she is plac'd; but she must also take her Part in common with the rest of her Sex, in sharing of the repeated Insinuations of those fluttering Coxcombs and others, that intrude themselves into most Families, to betray the young and beautiful. Hence that just Observation of Dr. *And—s—n*, delivered from his Pulpit, *viz.* "That of *twenty* reputed Virgins, scarce *seven* carry their Maiden-heads to the Marriage-Sheets."

There are, indeed, some virtuous old Ladies, who knowing by Experience, how dangerous it is, for a pretty Girl to breed before she is betrothed, do therefore keep Hawks Eyes upon their Daughters, in whom, they see themselves at Sixteen, and will not let a young Lady stir a Foot abroad without a Footman at her Heels: *Our John* may carry a harmless *North-Country* countenance, and look as simple as a Man that is just married; yet, if Miss and his Waters are not narrowly watch'd, he may chance to make an irreparable Breach in a young Creature's Character, and of which we have had but too many Instances.

I remember, a beautiful *Blossom*, an Apprentice in *Lombard-Street*, whom her friends had strong reasons to suspect had met with *Male treatment*, or according to the Phrase, *had been dabbling*; and who for obtaining Satisfaction, got her examin'd, touching the Premises, by one of the most skilful Man-Midwives in *London*: The *Doctor* assur'd them, and moreover, offer'd to give it under his Hand, that the Girl was as unspotted a Spinster, as any we had in *Great Britain.* Her Relations went off perfectly well satisfied, and continued so for about two Months, when our immaculate *Milliner* was safely brought to Bed of a fine young *Silver-Smith*.

It is a certain Maxim among our experience'd Whore-masters, when they are in Pursuit of a pretty Wench, to make a narrow Inspection into the lower Part of her Garb; a more than ordinary Nicety about the Heels, with a violent Passion for fine clean under Petticoats, gives them pretty sure Hopes of securing their Game: while a Slattern with a dirty Pair of Shoes and Stockings, and a draggl'd Tail, generally proves an inflexible Hussey, and holds them out beyond all degrees of Patience.

Those judicious Matrons, Mrs. *D———*, and Mrs. *H—yw—d*, have often commiserated the Conditions of many little dirty Sluts, that have stood idle in the *Marketplace*, pinch'd with Hunger and half naked, whom a *tight Pair of Stays*, or even a *second hand Silk Night-Gown*, might have render'd *useful to their Country.*

I have frequently smil'd, to see a debauch'd *Veteran*, Ogling a fine Woman at Church, and taking a View of the Fortifications. Some Women are naturally more chaste, or rather, to speak properly, less amorous than others, and at the same Time have very strict Notions of Honor. Such women are almost impregnable, and may be compar'd to Towns strongly fortified both by Art and Nature, which, without Treachery, are safe from any Attacks, and must be reduc'd by long and regular Sieges, such as few Men have the Patience and Resolution to go thro' with; Unless their Charms are great indeed, sufficient to provoke Men to be at any tolerable Pains and Cost, and then their Chastity can never hold out long, but must infallibly surrender.

Others, who have a very moderate share of Honour, join'd to a very amorous Constitution, their Virtue is intirely Defenceless; and as soon as a Man has remov'd that little timorous Coyness, which is natural to young Women in their first Attempts, he may proceed with Confidence, and conclude the Breach to be practicable; for, what-ever Resistance he meets with afterwards, will only enhance the Pleasure of Conquest. Most Women, indeed, let them be ever so fully resolved to comply, make as great a shew of Resistance as they can conveniently counterfeit; and this the Sex would palm upon the World for a kind of innate Modesty.

Not to mention the actual Pleasure of a Woman receives in struggling, it is a Justification of her, in the Eye of the Man, and a kind of *Salvo* to her Honour and Conscience, that she never did fully comply, but was in a Manner forc'd into it. This is the plain Reason, why most Women refuse to *surrender* upon Treaty, and why they delight so much in being *storm'd.*

Hudibras has ludicrously plac'd the Seat of Male Honour in the Posteriors, whereby it is secur'd from any Attack in Front; but Female Honour, notwithstanding the apparent Safety of the Situation, like a Debtor's House upon the Verge of two Counties, is liable to be attack'd both ways, à Parte ante, & à Parte post.

In short, these Things rightly consider'd, it can no longer be wonder'd at, that Men shew so little Inclinations to marry, when they see a *Maidenhead*'s as easy to be obtain'd as a *Peace-Warrant,* and the other one granted upon a *single Oath,* as well as the other.

A *Stay-maker* at St. *James*'s assures me, that he never waits upon a certain Peeress, to make Proof of his Art, but that she puts him as much out of Countentance, as a young Lady who hath had the Misfortune to *break Wind* before her Admirer.

Singing-Masters, Dancing-Masters, and *Linnen-Drapers,* are for ever boasting of the mighty Temptations they have withstood in the great Families that have requir'd their Attandance; but I don't remember to have read of many *Josephs* in the Fraternities of the two former.

Notwithstanding the Maxim of our discreet Matrons, "That 'tis better for a young Wench to smart than itch:" I cannot help thinking, that the initiating of our Urchins so early in the ancient Science of Copulation, hath been attended with

very ill Consequences, and been productive of many growing Evils. It hath set all our hanging-sleeve Ladies a hankering
for a more substantial Food than Bread and Butter; and there
have been Instances of Parents, who have presented their Children so very young at the Altar, that the Ministers have been
about to perform the Office of *Baptism*, instead of the Rites of
Matrimony. Besides, it hath occasion'd the loss of a very con-
fidential Branch of *Trade*, and even prov'd detrimental to the
Revenue, for 'tis become a great Rarity to see a *Doll* among the
more innocent Amusements of our *young Gentry*, who are now
truly grown wise enough, to prefer *big Bellies* to *jointed Babies*.
My worthy Friend Mr. *Deard* tells me, that to exhibit such
a foolish Emblem in his Shop to a girl of ten or eleven Years
old, would be one of the greatest Indignities he could offer to
a young Virgin Customer, and which could not fail drawing
down the Resentment of the Miss's Mama, who wou'dn't take
it over-kind in him, to teaze her Child with the dry Represen-
tation of what she thinks herself capable of enjoying in Perfection; especially when she knows her Daughter is desirous and
pretty enough to be made pregnant as soon as other Children.

Nor can there be a more ridiculous Custom, than to set
up a *young Thing* scarce out of leading-strings, in the richest
of *Silks* and *Linens*, dish'd out like a Bride in the most delicious Manner, with *Lace, Essence,* and *Ribbons*, as though she
was going to be led to a Couch instead of a Cradle. There
are Women whose wonderful Sagacity will justify this strange
Conduct, in the remote Prospect of a Match, fancying all this
will make an early Impression upon some little Master they've
got their Eye for Miss: But I have known them by these Artifices, oftener catch a *Tartar* than a *Husband*.

The boundless Pride and Extravagancy or others, in dressing out their Daughters of riper Years, so vastly beyond what

their Circumstances are able to support, is another chief Reason why our Stews are so plentifully supplied with *Women*. It is fitting a Child out like a *Sallee-Rover* with *false Colours*, to cruise upon the Publick, and make *lawful Prize* of any Fool of Fortune, who is ready to die at the Sight of a new Manteau.

Now and then a raw inconsiderate Booby, whose Eyes have been more intent upon a suit of *Paduasoy* or *Pinners*, than a *Pulput*, hath been taken suddenly ill, and oblig'd to leave the Churhc in the Midst of Divine Service; his friends finding out the Cause of his *Malady*, apply to the *fine Lady's* Father. *Why truly I cannot but say I like the young Gentleman well enough, but I have been at vast Expences in bestowing an Education on my Daughter; the Child, I bless God for it, knows how to behave and* dress *herself, as well as e'er a* Duchess *in the Land; and though I say it that shou'd not, she can read a* Play *and dance a* Minuet *to Admiration. I have large* Sums out, *'tis true, therefore cannot as present advance any* Great Matters, *till it shall please God to call me, and then there's but she to* enjoy all *I have been carping for my Life-time.*

The Boy by this Time, is got into the first Stage of a Consumption, and his indulgent Parents, willing to save a Child's Life, and prevent an unhappy young Woman's falling into the Jaws of the Town, condescends to make a Match on't, upon Condition, that only five righteous Hundred Pounds can be found in the Family for her Portion. These are trying Circumstances, *Lucifer* can be as soon rais'd as a third Part of the Money: The Business breaks off, and none but the silent World is let into the Secret, by which the poor Girl is put beyond the Possibility of getting a Match, and at last submits to a lewd Amour. Thus she, who the other Day was thought in a Condition to make her Fortune, *is now upon her Country.*

There is hardly a Village within twenty Miles round *London*, but affords a kind Residence to one or more *Widows*, who have had *Husbands,* to whom they had the Misfortune to be never *married*, and who by being tied down to certain yearly Stipends, (the Wages of their *youthful Labours,*) are oblig'd to pass the latter Part of their Days in a retired Manner. If such a one has a Female Pledge of her *conjugal Love* left, she hath however this Consolation, that if it please the L———d to spare the Child's Life, and she turns out with any Thing of a Shape and Face, she may one Day prove a delicious Morsel for a Man of Quality, and so by getting into comfortable keeping, be able to support the Grey Hairs of her Mother in Affluence to the Grave.

The *natural Issue* of the Nobility, Clergy and Gentry of this Land, make at present no inconsiderable Part of the *Beau Monde*, Bastards beget Bastards, and spurious women Women bring forth spurious Daughters. We have before our Eyes lineal Descents, and regular Offsprings or Bastardy, which seem to be in as sure and happy a Way of being handed down to futurity, as a publick-spirited Whore-Master (regardful of Posterity) can wish for.

The Progeny springing from the merry Beds of Marriages, *during Good-pleasure*, face the World with a *bon grace*, appearing at all Assemblies and publick Diversions, with as much Credit and Lustre as the most legitimate Looby of us all.

Some Years ago, the Inhabitants of a certain Parish between *Temple-Bar* and St. *James*'s were severely pelted from the Pulpit with Discourses against the abominable Whoredoms suppos'd to be committed within their Walls' at length, their Minister dying, they thought of a notable Expedient for extricating their Ears out of this Difficulty, by wisely choosing for their Lecturer, a Gentleman who had married a Lord's Bastard Daughter.

I have e'er now seen a whole Congregation put to the Blush, when a *Reverend Gentleman* has been pleas'd to prostitute the Prayers of the Church, by way of a Compliment to his *Right Honourable Master*, whom almost every one in the Place had reason to believe, to have been at that very Instant in Bed between a Brace of Harlots.

Passing by a Bagnio one *Sunday* Morning, I was not a little surpriz'd, to hear a fine personable Man, drest in a rich Suit of lac'd Cloaths, and taking Chair, give Orders to be set down at the Parish Church; while the Gentlewoman of the House, who waited on him to the Door, charg'd the Chairmen to proceed with the utmost Expedition, because it was a Case of Necessity, the Gentleman beingn oblig'd to be timely there, to *Qualify* for a considerable Post in the Army.

There are some rich generous Sinners who in the Winter of their Leachery, only keep a Wench for the Pleasure of now and then obliging a Bottle Companion. A *Madam* once shew'd me a *Draught* that her *Friend*, as she affected to call him, had just made upon her; and having obtain'd a Copy, I thought I could do no less than oblige my courteous Readers with it.

August 23, 1748.

Dear MOLLY,

On Sight hereof permit the Bearer, to immediately enter a Pair of Holland *Sheets with you; let him have Ingress, Egress and Regress to your Person, in such Manner as to him shall seem meet, for the Space of twenty-four Hours, and no longer, and place it to the Account of*

	Your kind and
King's-Arms *Tavern,*	Constant Keeper,
Four in the Afternoon	EDMUND EASY.

P.S. *Child go through all your Exercises and Evolutions, as well for your own as my Credit.*

One day beign at Dinner with an Acquaintance at his House, in a little *Bye-street* near as *Red-Lyon Square*, some-body knock'd as *solitarily* as an *Undertaker* when he comes with his Compliment of Condoleance: The Door opening, a Female Voice ask'd to *see the Lodgings*, a fine young Creature genteely dress'd, attended by a Woman four times her Age, indifferently habited, was introduc'd into the Entry. As they pas'd by the Dining Room, in which was much Compay, the Lady started back; but recovering the *Surprize*, and with the Help of her *Fan*, she advanc'd to the Stairs Feet, where we could hear the want of a *Back-Door* lamented as a very great Misfortune attending the House; great Enquiry was made what sort of a *Neighborhood* it was, whether there were any *gossiping* and prying *People* in it, and what kind of *Lodgers* were already in the House? An *opposite Row* of *Houses* was complain'd of, as an intolerable Inconvenience, because *Madam* said, that if her Friend lik'd the Lodgings, and they could agree in the Price, the People would find themselves very happy in their IN-MATE, who would occasion very little trouble, by reason her *Spouse*'s Employment did not permit him to come home above *two* or *three* Nights in a Week. Presently the good Woman of the House return'd to the Table in tip-top –spirits, telling us she had lett her first Floor to a Male and Female, to do the Work of Creation in without a Licence from the Clergy: But what must one do, adds the Woman, how should People be able to pay their Rent ad Taxes, if they were to be over-scrupulous in such Matters; especially, when half the Lodgings within the Bills of Mortality are fill'd with *Coiners of false Love?*

But what amazes and fills all Mankind with Wonder and Surprize, is a *new Vice* started upon us, introduced and bold-ly led up by Women of the first Figure and Fortune as well as

Fashion, worthy the Imitation of the whole Sex. These, *vice versa*, have inverted the Order of Things, turn'd the Tables upon the Men, and very fairly begin openly to *Keep their Fellows*: For Ladies during the Bands of Wedlock, as well as in a State of Widowhood, to call in private *Aid, Assistance* and *Comfort*, is an Immunity they've enjoy'd time immemorial: But for the *Fair*, and such as even profess Spinsterhood, to keep Men in private Lodgings, and visit them publickly in their Equipages, are Privileges unknown to our Ancestors.

I don't know indeed how far the *Sex* may value themselves upon this notable Discovery, which perhaps they may fancy to be a just Method or Reprisal; but all sober considering People will look upon the Thing, as it certainly is, a most enormous Sin to lay Snares for the Unwary, and be the Means of ruining both Souls and Bodies of many innocent young Gentlemen: to which, however, I hope, the Wisdom of the Nation will put a speedy and effectual Stop, otherwise it will be no difficult Matter to foresee what infinite Numbers of Men must inevitably be made miserable.

A young Fellow of six Foot, and every Way proportionable, was the other Day enquir'd after at the *Temple Exchange*. The People of the House said, they had not seen him for some time, but heard he was in extraordinary *good Keeping,* and went but seldom abroad. I have my Eye at this time, upon several strapping Blades, who are like-wise upon this Establishment.

It is said indeed, that some of these unhappy *Wretches* have the Foresight and Discretion, before they'll venture to part with one *Inch* of their *Virtue*, to obtain some sort of Settlement or other, and not altogether depend on the fine Speeches and fair Promises of a capricious Woman, who perhaps in two or three Weeks after Enjoyment, or upon sight of a new Face, may take it into her Head to turn a poor deluded Fellow *upon*

the Common. We had the other Day, a cruel Instance of a pretty *dapper Boy*, who was wickedly seduc'd away from School,
by a *Lady*, whose Years, Education and Fortune, might have
taught her more Grace, than to have been the undoing of an
innocent young Creature; for such was his unhappy Case, she
having no sooner satisfied her brutal Appetite, and he acquir'd
some Reputation in her Service, but the Lad lost his Bread, for
only measuring one Inch and three Quarters less between the
Shoulders, than his Rival.

Though it must be confes'd that the Conduct of some of
these *poor Devils*, like that of the *other Sex*, will admit of no
manner of Justification, when their Extravagancies have no
Bounds, and when they shew a ready Disposition to prostitute
themselves to every Raking *Slut* that falls in their Way such a
Behaviour indeed, hath not only abus'd, but justly forfeited
the Affections of a kind *Benefactress.*

A hard Case happen'd the other Day to one of these *Kept
Masters*, who was turn'd off after five Months faithful Services,
for not regarding the frequent Admonitions given him, to forbear the Use of *Coffee* and *Tobacco*, with other Things of an
absorbing and *emaciating* Quality.

But there was an Instance of nice Honour, the last Season
at *Tunbridge*, where a well-siz'd *Hibernian*, who is retain'd by
a certain great *Duchess*, had the Virtue to resist a corrupt Officer made to him by a Baronet's Lady; who, according to a
common Fame, accosted him with a Purse of a hundred Pieces
in it: but the honest Gentleman declar'd, that his Conscience,
for ten times that Sum, wou'dn't suffer him to be guilty of so
manifest a Wrong to his *Keeper.*

There goes a Report, though God forbid it should be true,
of a certain rich *Mercer* in this great and opulent City, whole
salacious Help-Mate hath acquired a Habit of dropping her

Handkerchief, when she hath a mind to single out one of her Husband's handsome Journeymen.

I must confess, that in the Business of Lust we ought to submit to the Ladies, and with Shame allow them the Preference; 'tis that can make *Sappho* witty; *Eloifa* eloquent; a country Wife politick; that can humble *Messalina*'s Pride to walk the Streets; can make tender *Hippia* endure the Severities of a Sea Voyage; can support the Queen of *Sheba* in a Journey to Solomon; and make *Thalestris* search out *Alexander* the Great. I cannot reflect upon the Stories of Semiramis's lying with all the handsomest Men in her Army, and putting 'em to death afterwards; of her offering her Son the last Favour; of Messalina the Empress prostituting her self in the publick Stews; and of Queen Joan of Naples providing a Bath under her Window, where she might see all the lustiest young Men naked, and take her Choice out of them; without admiring the Actions of our ancient as well as modern Heroines in the Manner they deserve. *Sappho,* as she was one of the wittiest Women that ever the World bred, so she thought with Reason, it would be expected she should make some Additions to a *Science* in which Womankind had been so successful: What does she do then? Not content with our Sex, begins *Amours* with her own, and teaches the Female World a new Sort of Sin, call'd the *Flats,* that was follow'd not only in *Lucian*'s Time, but is practis'd frequently in *Turkey,* as well as at *Twickenham* at this Day.

But omitting those whose Actions are recorded to their Infamy, let us see a little of those who are cry'd up for the Glories of their Sex. And who more cry'd up amongst 'em than *Judith*? What Action more celebrated, than her murdering *Holofernes,* when he had treated her with all the Kindness and Respect imaginable in his Tent? For my Part, I must own, my Virtue does not arrive to so high a Pitch, and should rather have suffer'd my Town to have been ruin'd, than have been guilty of an Action that appears to my so barbarous: but I confess, that of *Jael* is yet worse, to invite a Man into her Tent, promise him Protection, and when he had trusted his Life in her Hands, to murder him whilst he was asleep. What shall we say to *Penelope*, who is instanc'd as a Pattern of Chastity and Conjugal Love? I will not with *Ovid* and *Virgil*, (if the *Priapeia* are his) make malicious Reflections upon her trying her Lovers Strength in a Bow; but take the Story as it lies in the *Odysses*, I am sure, she would hardly pass for such a Saint in our Days. And if a Lady had her House full of Lovers for twenty Years of her Husband's Absence, and if her Husband were forc'd to fight all these before he could have his Wife again, 'tis possible the Lampooners of the Town would not have represented her Case so favourably as *Homer* has done. But what shall we say to *Lycrophon*, even amongst the *Greeks*, who speaks of her as a most profligate Woman; or to D*uris Samius*, who asserts her to have been so very common, as to have kept open ———— to all Comers and Goers during her Husband's Absence, from whose promiscuous Copulations *Pan* was born, and therefore took the Name *Pan*, which in *Greek* signifies *All*. For *Lucretia*, I shall not insinuate, as a great Wit seems to do, that she stabb'd herself rather than return to the Embraces of a Husband, after having been so much better pleas'd by a Callant; but if she were one that valu'd her Chastity so much , and her Life so little, as they wou'd make us believe, 'tis somewhat odd, that she should rather let *Tarquin* enjoy her alive, than a Slave lie in the Bed with her when she was dead; and that she shou'd chuse to commit the Sin, rather than bear the Shame.

But let us forgive 'em all these Things, I have mention'd, since there is no Beauty in a Woman but what is a Sign of some Vice; let us attribute it to Nature's Fault, not theirs, and reckon that the more vicious they are, the nearer they come to the Perfection of the Sex.

The Tricks of *Bawds* and *Jilts*, two Ranks of degenerated Animals, so exactly impious, so solemnly and deliberately vicious and scandalous, that their very Names, the very Title of a *Bawd* and a *Whore*, is sufficient to fright a sober Man, not only from their Embraces and Conversation, but even out of all manner of lustful Thoughts and Inclinations. In the first Rank, I place the *Bawd* or *Procurer*, you may call her what you will; for though the latter has usurp'd a Name a little more Modish and Decent than the former, and perhaps may have a little more Business among the *Quality* and *Gentry*, yet they are both Practitioners in the very same Arts and Sciences, and constantly agree in the Main of their Occupation; there's no Difference that ever I heard between Mother ————*n*, and Mother————*r* , or my Lady K———— either, only in Point of Price, the one will equip you for a *Crown*, while the other won't do it under a *Guinea*, and perhaps not warrant the Goods found in the Bargain.

There are Creatures ever running into Families, under Pretence of selling *Teas* and other *India g*oods, that are laying Snares and Temptations, to entangle and betray young Women of small Fortunes, and Wives of Wanton Dispositions: Sometimes they'll have the delicatest Woman in the World for you, at other Times a fine young Creature of about Fourteen, a perfect Pattern of Innocence and Modesty, and a pure Virgin; besides, she has one that sings like an Angel; another that dances to a Miracle; a third that has an incomparable Shape and Mien; and a fourth, that's an absolute Wit, and the only diverting Mistress of her Sex.

When a Man, at the Expence of two or three hundred Pounds, has got himself mounted upon a fine young Harlot, she will stand him in five times as much in a Year's Keeping, as a Race-Horse or two, and who's Stable of Hunters together. She must be kept finely cloath'd and nicely drest, and have good Meat in her Belly and something beside, or else she'll immediately turn Jade upon him.

> When first the *Milk-maid* puts her Charms to Sale,
> Of Silk and *Flanders* Lace does seldom fail;
> With fine Gold-Watch; and Lodgings near the Court;
> She treats with Beaus, and makes our Nobles Sport,
> Shines out the first at ev'ry publick Place,
> And from the Play is handed by his *Grace*;
> Pursues exactly all the Gentry's Ways,
> Like them she runs in Debt, —like them she pays;
> Like them she paints, (delightful Beauty's Vail)
> And turns her honest Red to Courtly Pale.
> Head of the Mode, —of ev'ry Club the Toast—
> She feeds her Grandeur at her Tradesmen's Cost.
> Fine Dames of Pleasure, (who disdain to hoard)
> Learn her to squander, what she can't afford.
> His *Lordship* teaches her to—keep her Word.
> Thus while her Purse is full, his *Lordship* kind,
> The blinded Creature never looks behind,
> To Reason deaf; will nought but Vice attend,
> Nor sees the Folly, nor yet dreads the End.
> Till Pleasure vanishes, and Griefs arise
> Her Wisdom growth as her Fortune flies;
> But *dear*'s the Knowledge, which Experience buys.
> Twice twelve Months spent in this gay thoughtless Life,
> She comes to Linnen Gown and round-ear Coif,
> And leaves her furnish'd Lodgings in *Pall-Mall*,
> Crying ——*kind* Bridges-Street *will do as well*;

Pawning her Watch, declares she has *been told,*
That *Pinchbeck's* Metal looks as well as Gold.
It is the Fashion too; at Court you find,
Few Ladies wear of any other Kind.
Each day a *Head*, a *Smock*, or *Suit of Cloaths,*
In sad Succession to the *Broker's* goes,
No more she shines with Nobles in the *Park*,
But takes a *City Prentice* for a spark,
Who robs the Till to make her Presents large,
And keeps his Harlot at his Master's Charge.
With *old* and *young*, with ev'ry Comer treats,
And just with all her Profit——poorly eats.
At length her Suits obtain'd, her Clients fail,
Nor can her Person, or her Wit prevail.
All weary, to some fresher Beauties stray,
Leaving the Wretch a whole Month's Rent to pay.
The cruel Landlord joyful at her Fall,
Turns her away, and seized on her All.
This unthought Blow, all Hopes of Joy defeats,
And gives a frightful Prospect of the *Streets*,
Where she must now the Midnight Sot regale
For Six-pence dry, and Six-pence spent in Ale.
Dejected thus, and overcome with Pain,
She seeks her last Resort in *Drury-Lane*;
Where rank Diseases on her Joys attend,
And only finds in Death a real Friend.

These Harlots at first play at a high Game, nothing will
serve some of them, less than a Settlement of *two or three Hun-*
dred Pounds per Annum, *a Coach, find Lodgings suitable for a*
Whore of Rank, and upon these Considerations, she'll be faithful to you, or at least she'll promise you she will: but this is

only a Promise *de Facto* neither; so long as your Estate lasts, and you can maintain her in her Extravagance and Grandeur; but when that fails, so does the Obligation too; she has the grand political Reasons ready, as well as the best Statesmen of 'em all, and commonly makes the same Use of 'em.

She can pray, cant, shed a few Crocodile Tears, or rather than fail, sham a Fit, as a Token of the Passion and Tenderness she has for you; but then your Back's no sooner turn'd, but she tells her *Stallion* you're a nasty, sickly, feeble Fellow, and that as soon as she has persuaded you out of the Settlement, and the new Furniture, she'll first affront you and then leave you.

If she finds you are a Cully indeed, and will be often impos'd upon by her, then she has a Thousand little wheedling Tricks and Artifices to decoy, and which she practices, even in the tender *Minute*; sometimes she's *breeding* forsooth, and then sure you cannot be so barbarous to *your own Flesh and Blood*, but you will take some Care of the *young One*; besides, she wants Night-Gowns, and Damask for Clouts, and a Thousand other Necessaries for a lying-in Woman.

There's my Lord *A*———*s*, and Sir *John B*———*s*, and Colonel *D*————*s* Misses, lay-in as much State the other Day, as the best Lady in the Kingdom; nay, Mr. F————, who is but an ordinary citizen, presented his Concubine with a Bed and the Furniture of a Room, that cost him above *two Hundred and fifty Pounds*; and what has she I wonder done, that she should not deserve as much the best of them? Why, sure's she's as handsome, and as young, and as capable of her Duty, as any of them, and do you think she'll be put off with your nasty shabby forty or fifty Guineas? No, truly, she rather thinks, that as Cases stand between you and her, you ought to cut off the Entail of your Estate, and settle a good Part of it upon her for her Life, and then let the Child heir it afterwards. And perhaps all this too may be Whore-craft and Pretences, and so she too must be forced (to bring herself off) to sham a Miscarriage, and that your Cruelty and hard-heartedness in not settling your Estate upon her, and answering her Demands, has been the Cause of it, and will at last force her to make away with herself. Well, but if you lov'd her as well as she loves you, you could not be so barbarous as to deny her any Thing.

Besides, she has been no chargeable Mistress to you neither; she has been your Drudge for at least these seven Months, and han't cost you fifteen Hundred Pound in the whole. If you had liv'd with some she knows in the Town so long, (but she is an easy Fool) 'twould have stood you in not a Penny less than three Thousand.

Their Tricks and Devices are numberless, and not to be paralell'd by any Thing but their Ingratitude and Inhumanity; there indeed they exceed themselves; nothing gin Nature, being so perfectly brutish and cruel as one of these kind of Creatures. The very moment you stop your Hand, they grow rude and insolent; and when they find you have entirely done in your Business, and turn'd you a grazing, who so ready as that very *Syren* that has spent your Estate, to laugh at, revile and scorn you; and you are not less her Buffoon now, than you were formerly in her Property.

To have done with her: A JILT IS A *Procurer, Bawd* and *Whore*, compounded together. A Vermin so ravenous and malicious, and withal so subtle and designing, so formally chaste and hypocritically virtuous, and yet so scandalously common and impudently lewd, so proud, and yet so mercenary, and above all, so insolently ill natur'd, that in the short Character of a *Jilt*, are comprehended all the Vices, Follies and Impertinencies of the whole Sex.

And lastly, for their Art of *trapping*, this is a Mystery that they commonly manage, either by the Assistance of a *pregnant Whore*, or by the Help or some Letters or Papers that they pick out of your Pockets, that gives them an Inlet into your Affairs. The first is carried on by *Procurers, Bawds* and *Jilts*, and the latter by *Sharpers, Setters* and *Bullies*: if they are once so fortunate to get a big-belly'd *Whore* into their Confederacy, then they carry her about in a kind of Triumph among all her *Cullies* and *Novices*; eveyr one under the Notion of being the true Father, must subscribe an individual Maintenance for the *Strumpet* and the *Brat*, or a Warrant must be got immediately, or the Overseers of the Parish call'd in to their Assistance to force you to it. 'Tis no matter to contest it, for if you do, they'll force the Woman to swear it upon you, and then your Reputation's lost, and withal you have the Charge of a *Whore* and a *Bastard* entail'd upon you *ad infinitum.*

Let a sober Person take a gentle Walk through the antient *Hundreds* of *Drury*, where ev'ry half a dozen Steps he meets with some off Figure or another, that looks as if the *Devil* had robb'd them of all their *natural Beauty*, which being in our Maker's Image, we derive from our Creator, and had infus'd his own infernal Spirit into their corrupt Carcasses; for nothing can be read but *Devilism* in every Feature; *Theft, Whoredom, Homicide* and *Blasphemy*, peep out of the very Windows of their Souls; *Lying, Perjury, Fraud, Impudence* and *Misery*, the only Graces of their *Countenance.*

One with *slip Shoes*, without *Stockings*, and a *dirty Smock*, visible thro' a *torn Petticoat*, yet with her Head dres'd up to as much Advantage, as if the Members of her Body were sacrific'd to all Wickedness to keep her ill-look'd Face in a little Finery. Another taken from the *Shoe-stool* or *Oyster-tub*, and put into *Whores Allurements*, she makes indeed a more cleanly Appearance, but becomes her Ornaments as a *Welch-Ale-Wife* doth a *Velvet Manteel*, or a *Sow* a *Hunting Saddle*. A third, at the Heels of a Porter hurrying to a Tavern, to sell Half a Crown's Worth of Fornication to a drunken Letcher.

Turn your Eyes up to the Chambers of Wantonness, and you behold the most shameful Scenes of Lewdness in the Windows even at Noon-day, some in the very Act of Vitiation, visible to all the opposite Neighbours. Others dabbing their *Shifts, Aprons,* and *Headcloths*, and exposing themselves just naked to the Passers by. A Gang of *Bailiffs, Butchers* and *Highwaymen* are drinking, and damning at an Ale-house Door, then every now and then out bolts a Fellow, and whips nimbly a-cross the Way, being equally fearful both of *Bailiff* and *Constable*, looking as if the Dread of the *Gallows* had drawn its Picture in his Countenance. Here and there a dirty shabby looking *Quack*, going from House to House to visit his rotten Patients, as publickly and openly as a Collector of the King's Tax; and as often call'd to from the Windows of the first to the third Story, to know how such an one goes on in her Salivation.

My Dear, will you give me a Glass of Wine; take me under your Cloak, my Soul, and how does your precious——— do? You hear at the Corner of every Court, Lane and Avenue, the Quarrels and Outcries of Harlots recriminating upon one another, Soldiers and Bullies intermixing, the most execrable Oaths are hears, such as the seldom exceeded, but at a *Stop* of *Carts* and *Coaches* in a Winter's Evening. By and by a Brandy-Shop is going to be demolish'd, because the Master refuses to bail some Whore that's just arrested, and a Coach waiting at the Door of her Lodgings to carry her to the Officer's House, unless he does the kind Office. A Riot breaks out in another Place, a Bawd's Goods are seized on for Rent; a new Tumult ensues, a Whore's Maid in crossing the Croud, has a Misfortune to break a Bottle of red Port, with a Couple of Pipes, that she is carrying to her Mistress's Chamber, the Mob give a Shout, the Girl is beat out of Doors with her Head bloody, all the Chandler-Women and Gin People are assembled, with an *Irish* Sollicitor at their Head about the Door, with an Outcry for *Justice*; poor *Peggy's* Rashness is blamed by some, and justified by others; in an Instant half a dozen Suits of Head Cloths are torn in Pieces, and several black eyes and bloody Noses exhibited: *Warrants, binding over,* and *Actions*, are the Subjects of all Conversation in *Coulson's-Court, Bridges-Streeet,* &c. A Cry of Murder is heard about twenty Yards farther, a *Mother* or *Father* being under the bastinading of a dutiful *Son* or *Daughter. Pimps* and *Pensioners* to the *Hundred*, you see sulking from Bawdy-House to Bawdy-House incessantly. In short, I cannot but fancy them a Colony of *Hell-Cats*, planted here by the Devil, as a Mischief to Mankind; they admit of no Comparison on this side Hell's Dominions, all this Part, quite up to *N—win—rs Lane, Park—rt'd Lsnr, Sc. Th—mas's-Street,* (some few honest Shopkeepers excepted) is a Corporation of *Whores, Coiners, Highwaymen, Gamesters, Pick-pockets*, and *House-breakers*, who like *Bats* and *Owls* sulk in obscure *Holes* and *Geneva shops* by Day-Light, but wander in the Night in search of Opportunities wherein to exercise their Villany.

An Inhabitant of this ancient *Sodom*, has inform'd me, that the eight Sessions of Oyer and Terminer, generally holden every year at the *Old Bailey*, together with the Act for the Transportation of Felons, had considerably lower'd the Rents in this Precinct, within a few Years, and greatly thinn'd the People, insomuch, that the half of some Streets and Allies were entirely depopulated; but, that the greatest Shock the Place ever receiv'd, was from the *Develian* Persecution, which had driven great Numbers of families out of their *Free-holds*, and scatter'd them all over the City and Suburbs, whereby the Trade and Business was chiefly remov'd to other Places, *viz.* the *Fourscores* of *Fleet-Street* and *Shoe-Lane*, the *Fifties* of *Dukesplace* and the *Minories*, and the *Course* of *Charing-cross*, which last was now render'd in as flourishing a Condition, as in the Reign of King *Charles* the IId, there being little else but Concubines in all the Lodgings, and nothing but *lascivious Looks* seen in the Chamber-Windows, from one End of the *Verge* to the other: Nor are very few of these the *Propriety* of *one Man*, but ordain'd for the *Comfort* and *Refreshment* of *Multitudes*, devoting themselves to the Service of ALL the loving Subjects of *Great-Britain*; such gay Volunteers give a young Fellow an handsome Prospect of the Town, leading him thro' all the *inchanting* Mazes, and even surfeit him with *Delight*, so that by the Time he is come out of their Hands, he is become very tame, and prepar'd for the dull Solemnity of *Marriage*.

There liv'd till about a Year ago, an elderly Woman, near *King-Street, Westminster,* who was every Day very needful in the World, yet every Day did a World of Mischief; who kept a House of free Hospitality, but made Folks pay vastly dear for what they had. But her Customers paid the greatest Price with the greatest Pleasure; for this celebrated Sinner dealt not in Trifles, such as *Wines* and *Ragousts*, but in Nervous Aches and Rottenness of Bones; she had always a Bible in her Hand at home, and always a to-be-ruin'd Damsel abroad; each Morning she took her Rounds to all the Inns, to see what Youth and Beauty the *Country* had send to *London* to make their Fortunes; and when she found a Rural pretty Lass step out of a Waggon, she drew her by her smooth Language to a private Box within, where, after telling the harmless Girl, *'twas pity such well-shap'd Limbs should twirl a Mop; such red and white Cheeks should be sullied with Cinders and Charcoal;*

such a ready Wit be subjected to the unreasonable Clamours of a bawling Mistress: This antiquated *she Captain* of *Satan*'s Regiment, would offer the poor innocent Creature an Apartment, all the Accommodations in her House *gratis,* till she saw if she should like the Town, f*or 'twas but a sad wicked Place, full of Temptations for young Girls, but the Almighty would deliver his good Children.* At other Times, she would go to the *Hospitals* and *Bridewel,* and pick out all the well-limb'd Creatures, these she's trick up with Patch and Paint, and lett out at extravagant Prices: always calling them young *Milliners* or *Parsons Daughters.* Indeed some shabby abandon'd Fellows, who us'd (for mercenary Ends) to smile at the old Matron herself, and chuck her under her wicked Chin, she'd relieve with a Supper, and sometimes afford them an After-Course, *viz.* some of her young Wares who appear'd to her the least Marketable. But such miserable Chaps as these (who tho' abandon'd by the World, could not abandon their Vices,) she did not much care for; observing, perhaps, with others, that the worse their Circumstances, the greater their Assurance.

If you meet with any of our Trading Madams, and ask them *who debauch'd her*, it is ten to one, but her Answer will be *Jack* ———— I have heard of above 500 unfortunate Women, who have laid their *Virginities* at the Door of this *young Gentleman.* At the latter End of Queen *Anne*'s Reign, a certain Viscount had the *Reputation* of *deflowering* far and near; the Elegance of whose taste was esteem'd such, that it was rather a Recommendation, than an Impediment to the Woman's *Marriage,* or her future *keeping,* if she had but once pass'd the *Hand* and *Seal* of Mr. *Secret—ry.* A merry but true Story, is related on that Occasion, *viz.* a Courtezan being met in the *Mall* by a Gentleman, he ask'd *whether she had heard the News* ———— *pray what is it?* ——*Why, your old Friend H——ry St.*

J——hn, is made S——c——y of Sl——e. What may that be worth, says the Lady——*Perhaps about* 1000 l. *a Year.* ——*By G—d I'm glad to hear it with all my Soul, for the Wh—res will get every Penny of it.*

In the *City*, every undone Woman lays her Ruin, t*o a Gentleman of the Temple*, but whether these Things are justly laid to their Charge, or whether it is only the Ambition of the *Jilt*, to have you think she sacrific'd her Virginity to the Use of so worthy a Society, I will not presume to determine; tho' I confess, I think it reasonable to believe, that our forward Ladies are more apt to dedicate their Honours to the *Inns of Court* than elsewhere, for three Reasons: *First*, as they are the Flower of our Gentry. *Secondly*, as the Greatness of their Number affords Variety of Choice. And, *Thirdly*, as they have the best Conveniences for comsummating Debauchery, without the Dread or Danger of Detection.

The greatest Evil that attends this Vice, or could befal Mankind, is the Propagation of that infectious Disease call'd the *French Pox*, which in two Centuries has made such incredible Havock all over *Europe*. In these Kingdoms, it so seldom fails to attend Whoring, now-a-days mistaken for Gallantry and Politeness, that a hale robust Constitution is esteem'd a Mark of Ungentility and Ill-breeding, and a healthy young Fellow is look'd upon with the same View, as if he had spent his Life in a Cottage. Our Gentlemen of the Army, whose unsettled Way of Life makes it inconvenient for them to marry, are hereby very much weaken'd and enervated, and render'd unfit to undergo such Hardships, as are necessary for defending and supporting the Honour of their Country; a remarkable Instance whereof happen'd the other Day near *Knightbridge*, where two Subalterns, *viz.* a *Lieutenant* with his Half-pike, and an *Ensign* with his Colours, were unhappily by a sudden Gust of Wind blown into a Ditch in their March to *Kensington:* And our Gentry in general, seem to distinguish themselves by an ill state of Health; in all Probability, the Effect of this pernicious Distemper. Nothing being more common, than to hear People of Quality complain of *rude vulgar Health,* and curse their *Porterly Constitutions.* Men give it to their Wives, Women to their Husbands, or perhaps their Children; they to their Nurses, and the Nurses again to other Children; so that no Age, Sex or Condition, can be entirely free from the Infection.

Another ill Effect, is, its making People profuse, and tempting them to live beyond that their Circumstances will admit of; for if once Men suffer their Minds to be led astray by this unruly Passion, no worldly Consideration whatsoever, will be able to stop it; and Wenching, as it is very expensive in itself, without the ordinary Charges of *Physick* or *Children*, often leads Men into a Thousand other Vices to support its Extravagance: Besides, after the Mind has once got this extravagant Turn, there naturally follows a Neglect and Contempt of Business, and Whoring of itself disposes the Mind to such a sort of Indolence, as is quite inconsistent with Industry, the main Support of any, especially of a Trading Nation.

The murdering of Bastard Infants is another Consequence of this Vice, but much worse than the Vice itself: And, tho' the Law is justly severe in this Particular, as rightly judging, that a Mind capable of divesting itself so entirely of Humanity, is not fit to live in a civiliz'd Nation; yet there are so many Ways of evading it, either by destroying the Infants before their Birth, or suffering them to die afterwards by wilful Neglect, that there appears but little Hopes of putting a stop to this Practice, which, besides the Barbarity of it, tends very much to dispeople the Country. And since the Prosperity of any Country, is allow'd in a great Measure to depend on the Number of its Inhabitants, the *Government* ought, if it were possible, to prevent any Whoring at all, as it evidently hinders the Propagation of the Species. How many Thousand young Men in this Nation would turn their Thoughts towards Matrimony, if they were not constantly desetroying that Passion, which is the only Foundation of it? And tho' most of them sooner or later, find the Inconvenience of this irregular Life, and think fit to confine themselves to one; yet their Bodies are so much enervated, by the untimely or immoderate Increase of this Passion, together with the Relicks of Venereal Cures, that they beget a most wretched, feeble, and sickly Offspring: We can attribute it to nothing else but this, that so many of our antient Families of Nobles are of late extinct.

There is one Thing more we ought to consider in this Vice, and that is, the Injury it does to particular Persons and Families; either by alienating the Affections of Wives from their Husbands, which often proves prejudicial to both, and sometimes fatal to whole Families; or else by debauching the Minds of young Women, a brutal Practice of too many of our intriguing Sparks, who make it a Piece of Gallantry, and the Qualifications of the *fine Gentleman*, to debauch young unguarded Innocents; and then after a plenary Gratification of their wild Desires, turn them loose to the wide World to get their Bread, by prostituting their Bodies to the Will and Embraces of every lewd Leacher, and distemper'd Bully, whence issue nothing but Infamy and a loathsome Disease; when the poor ruin'd Damsel would never have sacrific'd her Honour, had she not strongly been deluded by a Thousand dreadful Imprecations, Vows, and solemn Oaths of future Marriage. These, and many of these there are, who have often confest this Truth with Tears: willing for ever to quit that infamous Commerce, could they otherwise subsist themselves, a Thing almost impossible they think, or hope for, after the irreparable Loss of Friends, Fame and Reputation. How often have I wish'd we had such a Provision for these unhappy Females, (and their Offspring) as they have in other Nations, who, tho' they are the Scorn and Contempt of the Generality of the unthinking World, are notwithstanding real Objects of our Pity and Compassion?

These are the several bad Effects of Whoring, and it is an unhappy Thing, that a Practice so universal as this is, and always will be, should be attended with such mischievous Consequences: But alas! this violent Love for Women is born with us, nay, it is absolutely necessary to our being born at all: And, however some People may pretend, that unlawful Enjoyment is contrary to the Law of *Nature*; this is certain, that Nature never fails to furnish us largely with this Passion, tho' she is often offering to bestow upon us, such a Portion of Reason and Reflection, as is necessary to curb it.

Publick Whoring consists in lying with a certain Set of Women, who have shook off all Pretence to Modesty; and for such a Sum of Money, more or less, profess themselves always in a Readiness to be enjoy'd. The Mischief a Man does in this Case, is entirely to himself; for, with respect to the Woman, he furnishes her with the Means of Subsistence. The Damage he does to himself, either with regard to his Health, or the Expence of Money, may be consider'd under the same View as Drinking, with this considerable Advantage, that it restores us to that cool Exercise of our Reaosn, which Drinking tends to deprive us of. But the Minds of Women are observ'd to be so much corrupted by the Loss of Chastity, or rather, by the Reproach they suffer upon that Loss, that they seldom or never change that Course of Life for a better; and if they should, they can never recover that good Name, which is so absolutely necessary to their getting a Maintenance in any honest Way whatever; and that nothing but meer Necessity obliges them to continue in that Course, is plain from this, that they defend themselves in Reality, utterly abhor it: And indeed, there appears nothing in it so very alluring and bewitching, especially to People who have that Inclination to Lewdness entirely extinguish'd, which is the only Thing could make it supportable.

The other Branch of Whoring, *viz. private*, is of much worse Consequence; and a Man's Crime in this Case, increases in proportion of the different Degree of Mischief done, if you consider his Crime with regard to the *Society*: for, as to personal Guilt, Allowance ought to be made for the Increase of Temptation, which is very considerable in the case of debauching *married Women;* upon the Account of the Safety to the Aggressor, either with respect to his Health, or the Charge, and, if that affects him, the Scandal of having a Bastard. On the other Hand, the Injury done is very considerable, as such an Action tends to corrupt a Woman's Mind, and destroys that mutual Love and Affection between Man and Wife, which is so necessary to both their Happiness. Besides, the Risque run of a Discovery, which at least ruins a Woman's Reputation, and destroys the Husband's Quiet; nay, where Virtue does not entirely give way, if it *warps* but ever so little, the Consequence is shockingly fatal: For, tho' the good Man's Suspicions of the Wife's Chastity; the Wife of the Gallant's Constancy, and the Gallant of the Husband's Watchfulness, by being a Check upon each other, may keep the Gate of Virtue shut; yet then, all Parties must be attended with a never-easing Misery, not to be imagin'd but by those who too fatally *feel it.*

Tho' there are a Sort of People about this Town, who please themselves with *Defamations*; one of these, if they see a Man speak to a Woman, make their *little Signs*, their *politick Winks*, and possibly, when they meet him, in their insipid way of Raillery, tax him with it: if he is angry with them, then he is piqu'd, and afraid the *Intrigue* should be *found out*; if he says nothing (and treats it as it deserves) then he is out of Countenance, and cannot *stand* it; and if he laughs at them, which is all the Answer a prudent Man would make to such Stuff, then he is pleas'd with the Thing: so that every way the poor Lady's *Reputation* suffers, and these Fellows shall not fail to blow it about the Town, that there is an *Amour*, not that they really think so of you, but that you may return the *Compliment*, and say the same Things of them when they are seen to speak to any *Lady* themselves.

The Next Thing that comes to be consider'd in this *Vice*, is the Expence it occasions, and the Neglect of worldly Business, by employing so much of our Time and Thoughts; for, let a Man have never so much Business, it cannot stop the Circulation, and the *Animal Spirits* will do their Office, let a Man's Thoughts be ever so much employ'd about other Affairs, that he cannot attend to every minute *Titillation*. A Man of Pleasure may indeed, make this *Copulative Science* his whole Study; and by his Idleness and Luxury, prompt Nature that Way, and spur up the Spirits to Wantonness: but then his Constitution will be the sooner tired; for the *Animal Spirits* being exhausted by this *Anticipation*, his Body must be weaken'd, and his Nerves relax'd; neither will his irregular effeminate Life assist them in recovering their former Tone: besides, those Parts which more particularly suffer the Violence of this Exercise, are liable to many Accidents, and Men of Pleasure, tho' otherwise pretty healthy, are often troubled with Gleets and Weaknesses, either by a former Ulceration of the *Prostrates*, or else some violent overtraining which occasions this Relaxation. These Men 'tis true, will talk very lusciously of Women; but, pretend what they please, they can never have that burning Desire which they had formerly, when all their Vessels were in full Vigor. The Truth is, their Lust lies chiefly in their Brain, kept alive by the Impression of former Ideas, which are not so easily rubb'd out, as the Titillation which created them, and this Passion comes to be so diminish'd, that in Time it changes its Residence. A Man of Business, on the contrary, or one who leads a sober regular Life, will seldomer be attack'd with these wanton Fits, but then they will come with double the Violence; for thought it is a common receiv'd Opinion, that the longer a Man refrains, the better he is able to refrain, yet it is only true in one Sense, and amounts to no more than this; that if a Man has been able for such and such Reasons to curb this Passion, for Instance, a Month, he will, if the same reasons hold, and without an additional Temptation, be able to curb it a Month longer; but, nevertheless, he may have Desires much stronger than a Man, who for want of these Motives to Abstinence, gratifies them every Day. If there are some Men of a particular Constitution, whose puny Desires may be easily block'd up, with the Assistance of *three small Buttons*, or else endow'd with such an extraordinary Strength of Reason, that they can master the most *rampant* Sallies of this raging Passion; I am here speaking of those Men of Business, who, notwithstanding their Abstinence, or the Regularity of their Lives, are sometimes prevailed upon to quench these amorous Heats; and I say, in such Men, the Passion is much stronger than in Men of Pleasure, and that their Abstinence contributes to heighten the Violence of the Desire, and make it the more irresistible: For, the Fancy not being cloy'd with too frequent Enjoyment, presently takes Fire; and the *Spermaticks* not being weaken'd with forc'd Evacuations, are in their full Vigour, and give the Nerves a most exquisite Sensation: so that upon the least toying with an alluring Wench, the Blood Vessels are ready to start, and to use *Othello's* Words, *the very Sense aches at her.*

Now what shall this Man do, when he has once taken the Resolution to be easy? He must either venture upon the Publick, where it is odds he meets with a Mischance, that will either drain his Pocket, and make him unfit for any Business, at least without Doors; or else he must employ both his Time and Rhetorick, and perhaps too his Purse, in deluding some modest Girl; which, besides the Loss of Time in carrying on such an Intrigue, is apt to give the Head such an amorous Turn, as is quite inconsistent with Business, and may probably lead a Man into After-Expences, which at first he never dreamt of.

Let us now consider the Affair of Matrimony. Since the World is now no longer in a State of Nature, but form'd into several Societies independent of one another, and these Societies again divided into several Ranks and Degrees of Men, distinguish'd by their Titles and Professions which descend from Father to Son; it is very certain, that Marriage is absolutely necessary, not only for the regular Propagation of the *Species*, and their careful Education, but likewise for preserving that Distinction of Rank among Mankind, which otherwise would be utterly lost and confounded by doubtful Successions. And it is no less certain and indisputable, that all Sorts and Kinds of Debaucheries whatever, are Enemies to this State, in so far as they impair the natural Vigour of the Constitution, and weaken the very Springs of Love. This necessary Passion is, indeed, of such a ticklish Nature, that either too much or too little of it is equally prejudicial, and the *Medium* is so hard to hit, that we are apt to fall into one of the Extremes. We are naturally *furnish'd* with an extraordinary *Stock* of Love; and by the *Largeness* of the Provision for *wear and tare.* If young Men were to live entirely chaste and sober, without blunting the Edge of their Passions, the first Fit of Love would turn their Brains topsy turvy, and we should have the Nation pester'd with Love-Adventurers, and Feats of Chivalry: By the Time a *Peer*'s Son came to be sixteen, he would be in danger of turning Knight-Errant, and might possibly take a *Cobler's* Daughter for his *Dulcinea*; and who knows but a sprightly young *Taylor* might turn an *Orlando Furioso*, and venture his Neck to carry off a Lady of Birth and Fortune. In short, there are so many Instances every Day of these ruinous disproportion'd Matches, notwithstanding our present Intemperance, that we may justly conclude, if the Nation was in a perfect State of Sobriety, no Man could answer for the Conduct of his own Children.

It must indeed be confes'd, as Matters now stand, the Excess of Chastity is not so much to be fear'd, as the other Extreme of Lewdness, tho' there are Instances of both; and many Fathers now living, would gladly have seen their Sons fifty Times in a Stew, rather than see them so unfortunately married. The other Extreme is equally or rather more danger-ous, as it is more common; for most young Men give too great a Loose to their Passions, and either quite destroy their Incli-nation to Matrimony, or make their Constitutions incapable of answering the Ends of that State.

When a Man and Woman select one another out of the whole Species, it is not meerly for Propagation; nay, that is generally the least in their Thoughts: What they chiefly have in View, is to pass the Remainder of their Lives happily together, to enjoy the soft Embraces and mutual Endearments of Love; to divide their Joys and Griefs; to share their Pleasures and Afflictions; and in short, to make one another as happy as pos-sible. As for Children, they come of Course, and of Course are educated according to their Parents Abilities.

Now all these Enjoyments depending upon the mutual Affection of these two, Man and Wife; whenever this Affection fails, either in the Woman of the Man, that Marriage is unhappy; and all the good Ends and Designs of this State entirely frustrated. To give the Women their due, they must have the Preference in Point of Constancy; their Passions are not so easily rais'd, nor so suddenly fix'd upon any particular Object: But when once this Passion is once rooted in Women, it is much stronger and more durable than in Men, and rather increased than diminished, by enjoying the Person belov'd. Whether it is, that Women receive as much Love as they part with and that the Love they receive is not entirely lost, but takes Root again by Conception; whereas what a Man parts with, never affects him farther than just the Pleasure he receives at the Time of parting with it; or whether the Difference is owing to the different Turns of Mens Fancies, which are more susceptible of fresh Impressions from every handsome Face they meet with, or perhaps, that their Heads are so much employ'd in worldly Affairs, that they only take Love *en passant*, to get rid of a present Uneasiness, whereas Women make it the whole Business of their Lives: Whatever the Reason is, I say, it is experimentally true, that a Woman has but a *slippery hold* of a Man's Affections after Enjoyment. Let us see therefore, which of the two, the chaste of the eperienc'd Man will be least liable to this Failure of Affection, and consequently, which of the two will make the best married Man.

The first great Cooler of a Man's Affections after Marriage, is the Disparity of the Match. When a Man has married entirely for Love, and to the apparent Detriment of his worldly Affairs, as soon as the first Flash of it is over, he can't help reflecting upon the Woman as the Cause, and in some Sense, the Author of his Misfortunes; this naturally begets a Coldness and Indifference, which by Degrees turns to an open Dislike. Now, it is these sort of Marriages that chaste Men are always in Danger of falling into, as I have already prov'd; neither is there any effectual Way to convince a Man of this Folly, and secure him against it, but by giving him some Experience. Again, as chaste Men seldom marry for any Thing but meer Love, so they have fram'd to themselves such high extravagant Notions of the Raptures they expect to possess, that they are mightily shock'd at the Disappointment. A chaste unexpereinc'd Man, is strangely surpriz'd, that those bewitching Charms should make such a faint Impression on him after a thorough Perusal; he can scarce believe that the Woman is still possess'd of the same Charms which transported him formerly; he fancies he has discover'd Abundance of little Faults and Imperfections, and attributed his growing Dislike to this Discovery, not dreaming that this Alteration is entirely in himself, and not in the Object of Desire, which remains still the same. The Truth is, when a Man is full fraught with Love, and that his Pulse beats high for Enjoyment, this peccant Love-Humour falls down upon the Eye, which may be observ'd at that Time to be full, brisk and sparkling: 'Tis then the Beauty of every Feature is magnified by coming thro' this false Perspective; for *Parthenope* will now appear to him a Mortal, such as she really is, divestes of all those false Glosses and Appearances.

The chaste Man is surpriz'd at this Chance, he is apt to lay the Fault upon the Woman, and generally forces his Affections on some other Female, who he imagines is free from Faults: then farewel happy Wedlock! The experience'd Man, on the contrary, has try'd several Women; he finds they all agree in one Particular, and that after a Storm of Love there always succeeds a Calm: when he enters into Matrimony, he is prepar'd against any Disappointment of that Nature, and is ready to make Allowance for those Faults and Imperfections which are inseparable from human Kind. This is so true, that Women have establish'd a Maxim, that Rakes make the best Husbands; for they are very sensible, how difficult it is to monopolize a Man's Affections; that he will have his Curiosity about those Affairs satisfied one Time or other: And tho' this Experience is useful before Marriage, it is very dangerous afterwards.

Besides, to compleat the Happiness of the Marriage-state, or indeed to make it tolerably *easy*, there must be some Agreements in the Temper, Humour and Disposition of the two Parties concern'd. If, for Instance, the Man can't endure the Sight of a *Metropolis*, and the Woman can't enjoy herself out of it; if the Man is grave, serious, and an Enemy to all jocular Merriment, when his Wife is a profess'd Lover of Mirth and Gaiety, these two can never agree; Differences will arise every Day, and Differences in Wedlock are as hard to reconcile, as those in Religion.

There is a Story of *Simonides*, that being ask'd about a Wife, he said, she was the Shipwreck of a Man, the Tempest of a House, the Disturber of Rest, the Prison of Life, a daily Punishment, a sumptuous Conflict, a Beast in Company, a necessary Evil. And *St. Chrysostom*, besides the Homily upon the beheading St. *John Baptist*, which is almost all an Invective against Women, says in another Place, What is a Wife? The Enemy of Love, the inevitable Pain, the necessary Evil, the natural Temptation, a desirable Calamity, a domestical Peril, a pleasing Damage.

EPITAPH,

On the greatest Whore-Master the last Century hath produced.

Here continueth to rot The Body of FRA——c——IS,
Who, with an INFLEXIBLE CONSTANCY, and
INIMITATABLE UNIFORMITY OF LIFE,

PERSISTED,

In Spite of AGE and INFIRMITIES,
In the Practice of EVERY HUMAN VICE;
Excepting PRODIGALITY and HYPOCRISY.
His insatiable AVARICE exempted him from the first,
His Matchless IMPUDENCE from the second.
Nor was he more singular in the
Un-deviating *Pravity of his Manners,* than
Successful in *accumulating* WEALTH,
For without TRADE or PROFESSION,
Without Trust of PUBLICK MONEY,
And without BRIBE-WORTHY SERVICE,
He acquired, or more properly created

A MINISTERIAL ESTATE.

He was the only Person of his Time
Who could CHEAT without the Mask of HONESTY,
Retain his primæval MEANNESS when possess'd of

TEN THOUSAND a YEAR.

And having daily deserv'd the GIBBET for what he *did,*
Was at last condemn'd for what he could not *do.*

Oh indignant Readers!

Think not his Life useless to Mankind!
PROVIDENCE conniv'd at his execrable Designs,
To give After-AGES a conspicuous PROOF and EXAMPLE
Of how small Estimation is EXORBITANT WEALTH
In the Sight of GOD, by his bestowing it on
The most UNWORTHY OF ALL MORTALS.

REASONS FOR THE Growth of Sodomy, &c.

CHAPTER I

*The general Contempt of Learning,
and Abuse in the Education of our Youth.*

Our Fore-Fathers were train'd up to Arts and Arms; the Scholar embellish'd the Hero; and the fine Gentlemen of former Days, was equally fit for the Council as the Camp; the Boy (tho' perhaps a Baronet's Son) was taken early from the Nursery and sent to the Grammer-School, with his Breakfast in his Hand, and his Satchel at his Back; subject to Order and Correction, he went regularly thro' his Studies; and, if tardy, spurr'd up: The School Hours over, and his Exercise made, he had his Moments of Play allotted him for Relaxation; then sought he the Resort of other Boys, either in the Fields, or publick Squares of the City; where he hard'ned himself against the Inclemency of the Weather, and inur'd himself to athletic Exercises; wholesome as well as pleasant: this has sent him home with his Blood in a fine Circulation, and his Stomach as sharp as a Plowman's; Supper over, and jogg'd down with t'other Frolick, he went to Bed and slept sweetly; after which he rose early the next Morning, fresh, and fit for Study, hurry'd on his Cloaths, and away to School again: No matter if his Hands and Face were now and then a little dirty, so his Understanding was clean: If his Cloaths were sometimes torn with some Skirmish, his Heart was whole, and the frequent Battles between School and School, (which were then in Vogue) inur'd him to Courage, gave him a Thirst after Honour, and a Proneness to warlike Exercises.

I would not from this have my little Hero esteem'd a Bully; no, his Learning temper'd his Passions; with all this Spirit, the Boy was bashful to the last Degree; dutiful and humble to his Parents, mannerly to his Elders and Superiors; he knew no Vice, being train'd up in a Series of Virtue; the Authors he read inspir'd him with Notions of Honour; the Heroes nad Sages, whose Lives he found transmitted with such Applause, through so many Ages, fill'd him with an Emulation to Knowledge, and a Thirst after Glory; familiarized to Temperance and Exercise, he was no Valetudinarian in his Constitution, but a Stranger to Debauch; and as he grew to his riper Years, where the virtuous Object of his first Wished crown'd his virtuous Love, there, in the Flower of his Health, and Vigour of his Yough, stampt he his Maker's Image: Behold our School-Boy now become a Father, blest with an endearing Wife, and a dutiful, beautiful Off-spring; his Love and Care for them, now makes him ready to pursue whatever State of Life Heaven has allotted him, his Abilities of Mind and Body, render him capable of serving his King, his Country, and his Family. His Application to Business keeps him from Debauch, and his Success so spurs him on, that he soon sees a fine Provision made for himself and Family; and his (perhaps small) Patrimony amply augmented; this shews the Advantages of a proper Education; I am sorry to say an old fashioned One.

Now let us take a Sketch of the modern Modish way of bringing up young Gentlemen.

Little Master is kept in the Nursery 'till he is five or six Years old, at least, after which he is sent to a Girl's School, to learn Dancing and Reading and , generally speaking, gets his Minuet before his Letters; for whereas Boys of old went to School at six in the Morning, and came home at eleven; Master goes at Eleven and stays 'till Twelve; for the poor Child must not get up till all its Things are aired, and 'tis barbarous to let him Breakfast without his Mamma; so that if he is drest by Tea-time, 'tis well enough: to let him have Milk-porridge, Water-gruel, or such like spoon Meats, is vulgar and unpolite; well, by eleven, or a little after Breakfast, is over, and Master taken to School, tho' very often Breakfast is drilled on till it is too late, unless they dance in a Morning, and then the whole Family is up sooner than ordinary. When he comes to School, he stands by his Mistress, who is generally working and looking another way all the while, he repeats the Alphabet after her not without some Interruption, tho' without the least Attention; for the Child is looking at its School-fellows, and the Mistress directing the young Ladies in their Samplers, or other fiddle faddles.

Here he continues till the Age at which Boys formerly went to the Universities, at last (with great Reluctance) he is sent to a Master, probably to a Writing School, for fear he should break his head with *Latin*; besides, *Grammar-Masters* are harsh; and the Child is of a tender Constitution: well may it be so, when the Tone of his Stomach has been spoiled with Tea, when his Blood is curdled with now and then a Dram, to keep the Mother in Countenance; when the Boy's Constitution is half torn to Pieces with Apothecary's *flip flops*, occasioned by early Intemperance, sitting up late on Nights, eating Meat *Suppers*, and drinking Wine, and other strong Liquors of most pernicious Consequence to Infant Constitutions.

Besides, his whole Animal Fabrick is enervated for want of due Exercise; and he is grown so chilly by over nursing, that he gets Cold with the least Breath of Wind; for, till he went to the *Girls School*, he seldom or never was out of the Nursery, unless to pay a Visit, in a Coach, with his Mamma: For, at the Mistress's *School*, he was brought up in all respects like a *Girl*, (Needle-works excepted) for his Mamma had charg'd him not to play with rude Boys, for fear of spoiling his *Cloaths*; so that hitherto our young Gentleman has amused himself with Dolls,

assisted at mock Cristnings, Visits, and other girlish Employ-
ments, inviting and being invited to drink Tea with this or
that School-fellow; insomuch, that his whole Life hitherto has
been one Series of Ignorance, Indolence, and Intemperance.

But here the Master being doubly bribed, by the Father to
bring him forward, and by the Mother not to *correct* him; with
much a-do, makes a shift to teach him to read and write a little
English, by which Time he is almost too big to go to School;
however, for form's sake, 'tis fit he should learn his Accidence
before he goes to the University, or to Travel.

The Boy, this spoil'd, becomes *Company* for none but
Women, and even of those, only the fantastical and impertin-
ent; for, to the Glory, as the latter are the Shame of their Age,
or Country.

When our youg Gentleman arrives to Marriage; I wish I
could say fit for it, what can be expected from such an enervated effeminate Animal? What Satisfaction can a Woman have
in the Embraces of this Figure of a Man? Should she at last
bring him a Child, what can we hope from so crazy a *Constitution*? But a feeble, unhealthy Infant, scarce worth the rearing
whilst the Father, instead of being the Head of the Family,
makes it seem as if it were govern'd by two Women: For he
has suck'd in the Spirit of *Cotqueanifin* from his Infancy: As
for supporting them, his Indolence won't let him undertake
any Thing laborious; his Ignorance denies him all Hopes of
any Thing of *Consequence*; and his Pride won't accept of what
is mean: (at least what he thinks so.) Thus, unfit to serve his
King, his Country, or his Family, this Man of *Clouts* dwindles
into nothing, and leaves a Race as effeminate as himself; who,
unable to please the Women, chuse rather to run into unnatural Vices one with another, than to attempt what they are but
too sensible they cannot perform.

CHAPTER II

The Effeminacy of our Men's Dress and Manners,
particularly their Kissing each other.

I am confident no Age can produce any Thing so
preposterous as the present Dress of those Gentlemen who
call themselves pretty Fellows: their Head-Dress especially,
which wants nothing but a Suit of Pinners to make them
down-right Women. But this may be easily accounted for, as
they would appear as soft as possible to each other, any Thing
of *Manliness* being diametrically opposite to such unnatural
Practices, so they cannot too much invade the Dress of the
Sex they would repent. And yet with all this, the present
Garb of our young Gentlemen is most mean and unbecom-
ing. 'Tis a Difficulty to know a Gentleman from a Footman,
by their present habits: The low-heel'd Pump is an Emblem
of their low Spirits; the great Harness Buckle is the Height of
Affectation; the Silk Waistcoat all belac'd, with a scurvey blue
Coat like a Livery Frock, has something so poorly preposterous, it quite enrages me; I blush to see 'em aping the Running Footman, and poising a great Oaken Plant, fitter for
a Bailiff's Follower than a Gentleman. But what renders all
more intolerable, is the Hair strok'd over before and cock'd
up behind, with a *Comb* sticking in it, as if it were just ready
to receive a Head Dress: Nay, I am told, some of our Tip top
Beaus dress their Heads on quilted *Hair Caps*, to make 'em
look more *Womanish*; so that Master *Molly* has nothing to
do but flip on his *Head Cloaths* and he is an errant Woman,
his rueful Face excepted; but even that can be amended with
Paint, which is as much in Vogue among our Gentlemen, as
with the Ladies in *France*.

But there is no *Joke* like their new-fashion'd *Joke Hats*, equally priggish and foppish; plainly demonstrating, That notwithstanding the *Bustle* they make about *Jokes*, they have them only about their *Heads.* But to see them dress'd for a *Ball*, or Assembly, in a *Party coloured Silk Coat*, is the Height of my Aversion: They had better have a *Mantua* and *Petticoat* at once, than to mince the Matter thus, or do Things by Halves.

But of all the Customs *Effeminacy* has produc'd, none more hateful, predominant, and pernicious, than that of the Mens *Kissing* each other. This *Fashion* was brought over from *Italy*, (the *Mother* and *Nurse* of *Sodomy*); where the *Master* is oftner *Intriguing* with his *Page,* than a f*air Lady.* And not only in that *Country*, but in F*rance*, which copies from them, the *Contagion* is diversify'd, and the Ladies (in the *Nunneries*) are criminally *amorous* of each other, in a *Method* too gross for Expression. I must be so partial to my own *Country Women*, to affirm, or, at least, hope they claim no Share of this *Charge*; but must confess, when I see two Ladies *Kissing* and *Slopping* each other, in a *lascivious Manner*, and *frequently* repeating it, I am shock'd to the last Degree; but not so much, as when I see two *fulsome* Fellows *Slavering* every Time they meet, *Squeezing* each other'd Hand, and other like i*ndecent Symptoms.* And tho' many Gentlemen of Worth, are oftentimes, out of pure good *Manners*, oblig'd to give into it; yet the Land will never be purged of its *Abominations*, till this *Unmanly, Unnatural* Usage be totally abolish'd: For it is the first *Inlet* to the detestable Sin of *Sodomy.*

Under this Pretext vile *Calamities* make their preposterous *Addresses*, even in the very *Streets*; nor can any thing be more shocking, than to see a Couple of *Creatures*, who wear the Shapes of *Men, Kiss* and *Slaver* each other, to that Degree, as is daily practiced even in our most publick Places; and (generally speaking) without Reproof; because they plead in Excuse, *That it is the Fashion.* Damn'd *Fashion*! Imported from *Italy* amidst a Train of other *unnatural Vices.* Have we not *Sins* enough of our own, but we must eke 'em out with those of *Foreign Nations*, to fill up the Cup of our *Abominations*, and make us yet more ripe for *Divine* Vengeance.

'Till of late Years, *Sodomy* was a *Sin*, in a manner unheard of in these Nations; and indeed, one would think where there are such *Angelic Women*, so foul a Sin should never enter in to Imagination: On the contrary, our *Sessions-Papers* are frequently stain'd with the Crimes of these *beastly Wretches*; and tho' many have been made Examples of, yet we have but too much Reason to fear, that there are Numbers yet undiscover'd, that this *abominable Practice* gets Ground ev'ry Day.

Instead of the *Pillory*, I would have the *Stake* be the Punishment of those, who in Contradiction to the Laws of *God* and *Man*, to the Order and Course of *Nature*, and to the most simple Principles of *Reason*, preposterously *burn* for each other, and *leave* the *Fair*, the *charming Sex*, neglected.

But as Loss of Appetite is inseparable from a feeble and depraved *Stomach*: so is this *Vice* most predominant in those, to whom *Nature* has been so sparing of her Blessings, that they find not a Call equivalent to other *Men.* And therefore, rather than expose themselves, they take the *contrary Road*; and, like Eunuchs, out of meer Madness and Disappointment, loath the dear Sex they have no Power to please.

This must be the Case, if we consider that the Majority of Persons suspected of this Vice, are antiquated Leachers; who have out-lived the Power of Enjoyment; are so conscious of their own Insufficiency, they dare not look a Woman in the Face.

But so numerous are they grown, it is high Time to put a Stop to them, lest the growing Generation be corrupted; and *England* rival *Italy*, in this most unnatural and wicked Practice.

No Step will be more effectual than at once to abolish the fulsome Custom of *Men Kissing* each other, and to admit of no Plea or Exception in Favour of so debatable a Practice.

Is not the old Custom of shaking Hands more manly, more friendly, and more decent? What need have we of *Judas* like a Practice? For my Part, I hold it so ridiculous foolish Custom for a Man to *Kiss* even his own Brother, it favours too much of *Effeminacy*, to say the best of it. I know some worthy Gentlemen so scrupulous, they will not on any Account *kiss* any Friend of Relation of the same *Sex*, and I saw myself, two Brothers take a very solemn Leave of each other without one *Kiss*, though not without Tears; and I dare say with more friendship than Ten Thousand *Kisses* could express. I am of a Society of Gentlemen, and with Pride I declare it; who have made a solemn Vow, never to give, or take from any Man a *Kiss,* on any Account whatever; and so punctual have we been in Observation of this Injunction, that many times at the Expence of a Quarrel, this Ryle has been most inviolably kept among us.

If such a Resolution was more universal, the Sons of *Sodom* would lose many *Proselytes,* in being baffled out of one of their principal Advances; for under Pretence of extraordinary Friendship, they intice unwary Youth from this first Step, to more detestable Practices, taking many Times the Advantage of their Necessities, to decoy them to their Ruin.

I know a Thousand Objections will be brought against what I say; I shall be laught at by all the Votaries of *Sodom* and Effeminacy; but I hope the manly and generous *Britons*, who yet survive, will take what I say into Consideration, and show themselves *Friends to the* FAIR SEX; by opposing all Inlets to the Sin of *Sodomy*, of which *Man-Kissing* is the very first.

With this, all other *Effeminacies* should be abolished; and each Sex should maintain its peculiar Character: I hope the

Ladies will not stand in need of any Advice from me; yet I could wish that some among them would seem less amorous of one another; for tho' Woman *Kissing* Woman, is more suitable to their natural Softness, and indeed more excusable than the like Practice in the contrary Sex; yet it ought to be done *(if at all)* with Modesty and Moderation, lest Suggestions, which I hope are false, and which to me seem improbable, should bring such Ladies under Censure; who give themselves too great Liberties with each other: for as the Age increases in Wickedness, new Vices may arise; and since they themselves see how fulsome it is in Gentlemen, I hope they will abstain *from all Appearance of Evil*, and contribute to the intended Reformation; not only by scorning and deriding such *Wretches* of *Men*; who shall openly affront them, by *Kissing* each other in their Presence: but that they will set the Gentlemen a Pattern, and shame them out of it by using a *Kiss*, if it must be used, in so decent a Manner, and with so great Restraint, that the most envious shall find no cause of Censure.

CHAPTER III

The Italian Opera's, *and Corruption of the* English *Stage, and other Publick Diversions.*

How famous, or rather how infamous *holy* has been in all Ages, and still continues in the odious Practice of *Sodomy,* needs no Explanation; it is there esteemed so trivial, and withal so modish a Sin, that not a Cardinal or Churchman of Note but has his *Ganymede*; no sooner does a Stranger of Condition set his Foot in *Rome,* but he is surrounded by a Crowd of *Pandars,* who ask him if he chuses a *Woman* or a *Boy*, and procure for him accordingly; this Practice is there so general, they have little else in their Heads or Mouths, than *Casto* and *Culo* which they intermix with almost every Sentence, (a beastly and withal a most stupid Interjection!) for, let them be talking on never so serious a Subject, these two Syllables must come in, though never so foreign to the Purpose; these they use just as the *French* do the Word *Foutre,* which must come in by Head and Shoulders in every Company and Sentence. Nay, there are those who will intermingle it Word for Word, to the no small Improvement of Conversation; we are not yet arrived to this Pitch of Perfection; but much may be hoped in Time: For since the Introduction of ITALIAN OPERA's here, our Men are grown insensibly more and more *Effeminate*; and whereas they used to go from a good *Comedy* warm'd with the Fire of Love; and from a good *Tragedy*, fir'd with a Spirit of Glory; they sit indolently and supine at an OPERA, and suffer their Souls to be sung away by the Voices of *Italian Syrens*; 'twas just the same in *Greece,* when they left their noble warlike Moods, and ran into soft Compounds of *Chromatic Musick*; of this the Philosopher complains, and to this attributes the Loss of so many Battles, and dwindling of the *Grecian Glory. Rome* likewise sank in Honour and Success, as it rose in *Luxury* and *Effeminacy*; they had Women Singers and Eunuchs from *Asia*, at a vast Price: which so softned their Youth, they quite lost the Spirit of Manhood, and with it their Empire. For they grew so *Womanish* in Mind, Gesture, and Attire; and withal so fearful of hurting their sweet Faces, which were nurs'd up with all the *Cosmetics* Art or Nature could invent or produce, that their Enemies kill'd 'em with their very Looks, and for fear of having their *Faces* gash'd, or their f*ine Cloaths* spoil'd, they turn'd their Backs upon those *ugly dirty Fellows,* and gave up their Liberty to preserve their *Effeminacy*. Heav'n grant the Application may never extend to *England*; but I leave any reasonable Person to judge, if the *Similitude* is not too close.

As the ITALIAN OPERA's have flourish'd, the *English* Stage has diminish'd. Where is that Life, Fire and Spirit which adorn'd our *Plays* of old? Look over the Productions of this last Age (MR. ADDISON's *Cato* excepted) and you will see nothing worthy to be call'd a *Play*, or proper to be exhibited to a *British* Audience: They are rather *Drolls* or *Farces*, than *Tragedies* and *Comedies*; so that it may well be said *Comedy* and *Tragedy* died with *Addison* and *Congreve*, and *Action* with *Booth* and *Oldfield.* Our *Players* are now turn'd *Ballad-fingers*; our *Theaters* are transform'd to *Pupper-shews*, improperly called *Pantomimes*; for the *Pantomimes* of the Antients were clever Fellows, that would exactly mimic, or imitate, the Voice and Gesture of any Man they had an Intent to *ridicule.* But in these *Pantomine Entertainments*, there is neither Head or Tail, Meaning or Connection: *Gods, Harlequins, Priests* and *Sailors,* are all jumbled together, even in *Temples*, in the most incoherent Manner, ten Times more extravagant than the most extravagant Dream that ever was yet dreamt: However, these *Drolls* have *crowded Houses*, while the best *Plays* of *Shakespear* are exhibited to *empty Boxes.*

This shews the Taste of the Town, and the Genius of the People; who, grown quite *Lethargic* with *Luxury*, and in a State of *Perdition*, dare not *think*, and only seek to be *diverted*.

The *Masquerades, Ridotto's,* and *Assemblies* of late so much the Mode, at once explain and condemn themselves. 'Tis the greatest *Reproach* imaginable to the *British* Nation, that they have suffered themselves to be bubbled at this rate by a Vagabond *Swiss*, who has liv'd *profusely* for many Years past, at the Expence of *English* Fools; a publick *Cock-Bawd*, who while others of his Profession have been punish'd by Justices, &c. has gone on with Impunity, caress'd by the Chief (I was about to say best) of our *Quality*; but for what Reasons may be easily imagined.

Next to the Abuse of *public Diversions*, is that of *private Conversation*, which is now reduced to these two important Heads, *tittle tattle* and *Quadrille*.

This *whiling* away of Time renders us such useless *Animals*, that we seem to live to no Purpose; for, as our *Senses* grow depraved, so will our *Appetites* and *Inclinations*: For it is evident to Men who have the free Use of their *Faculties*, that as there is no Pleasure on Earth equal to the Possession of an *agreeable Woman*; so it must be confess'd, that whoever runs into any *Extreme* of a contrary Nature, it is because he is neither *worldly* or *capable* of enjoying so great a *Blessing*.

CHAPTER IV

*The Persecution of Prudes, and Barbarity
of* Women *one to another*

Now I have given the *Gentlemen* due Discipline, the *Ladies* must excuse me if I caution them against the malicious Insinuation of *Prudes*, whose Pride is to demolish every one's *Character* to set up their own, when at the same Time they themselves are most voluptuous private *Libertines*, sinning with the utmost Secrecy and Security, and yet are maliciously prying and magnifying into *Crimes*, every little unguarded Liberty taken by *unwary Persons*, who, too secure in their good *Intentions*, are oftentimes represented as *Devils*, by these much greater *Devils*, whose only Aim is to blacken whatever *Reputation* is fairer than their own.

An old Proverb says, *There is no Harm done where a good Child's got.* Faults of this Nature must be confess'd to proceed from a Richness in *Constitution*, and therefore, are more excuseable than *base* and *unmanly Practices.* It is the Action of a *Man* to *beget* a *Child*, but it is the Act of a Beast, nay worse, to———I scorn to stain my Paper with the Mention; but how many too fearful Persons are there, who dread more than the Scandal of a Child, than the Charge? How many Murders have been committed! How many innocent Babes have perished by Parish Nurses, because their Fathers have not had Fortitude enough to stand the Shock of common scandal? Many Men having but too often seen their own Flesh and Blood starv'd to Death, and their Estates left to Strangers. I write not this to encourage *Licentiousness*, but to alleviate the Thing, when an irrecallable *Accident* has happen'd. Let us suppose a *Man* and *Woman* in the Flower of their *Youth*, passionately fond of each other, indulging themselves in the utmost Latitude of Love; admit the *Woman* become *pregnant*, must she be exposed, stigmatized, eternally ruin'd for this *slip*? Must the *Man* be turn'd out of all Business, and banish'd Society for loving a Woman? Must the poor innocent *Babe* be deem'd an *Outcast*, upon whom Almighty GOD has thought fit to stamp his *sacred Image*?

If 'tis a Sin to *beget* a *Child*, 'tis a much worse not to *provide* for it; it 'tis a Sin to *debauch* a Woman, 'tis a much worse to *expose* her; if 'tis a Sin for a Man to *love* a pretty Girl; 'tis a much worse to *burn* her for his own Sex.

Let then the *Ladies* be more *merciful*, the *Gentlemen* more *manly*. Let a Harmony between the two *Sexes*, and an universal Charity (the greatest of *Perfections*) reign among us, teaching us to walk in the Paths of *Virtue* ourselves, without being so uncharitably *vain-glorious* of our own Merits, to lose all Compassion for the *venial Offences* of our fellow Creatures.

CHAPTER V
Of the Game of Flatts.

I am credibly informed, in order to render the Scheme of Inquity still more extensive amongst us, a new and most abominable Vice has got footing along the W———n of Q———y, by some call'd the Game at Flats; however incredible this may appear to some People, I shall mention a Story from an Author of very great Credit, applicable to the Matter, who, speaking of the *Turks*, says,

"A *Turk* hates bodily Filthiness and Nastiness, worse than Soul-Defilement; and, therefore, they wash very often, and they never ease themselves, by going to Stool, but they carry Water with them for their Posteriors. But ordinarily the Women bathe by themselves, bond and free together; so that you shall many Times see young Maids, exceedingly beautiful, gathered from all Parts of the World, exposed naked to the View of other Women, who thereupon fall in Love with them, as young Men do with us, at the Sight of Virgins.

By this you may guess, what the strict Watch over Females comes to, and that is not enough to avoid the Company of an adulterous Man, for the *Females* burn in Love one towards another; and the Pandaresses to such refined Lovers are the Bards; and, therefore, some *Turks* will deny their Wives the Use of their public Baths, but they cannot do it altogether, because their Law allows them. But these Offences happen among the common sort; the richer sort of Persons have Bathes at home, as I told you before.

It happened one Time, that at the public Baths for Women, an old Woman fell in Love with a Girl, the Daughter of a poor Man, a Citizen of *Constantinople*; and, when neither by wooing nor flattering her, she could obtain that of her which her mad Affection aim'd at, she attempted to perform an Exploit almost incredible; she feign'd herself to be a Man, changed her Habit, hired an House near the Maid's Father, and pretended he was one of the *Chiauxes* of the *Grand Seignor*, and thus, by reason of his Neighborhood, she insinuated herself fin to the Man's Acquaintance, and after some Time, acquaints him with the Desire of his Daughter. In short, he being a Man in such a prosperous Condition, the Matter was agreed on, a Portion was settled, such as they were able to give, and a Day appointed for the Marriage; when the Ceremonies were over, and this doughty Bridegroom went into the Bride-chamber to his Spouse; after some Discourse, and plucking off her Head-geer, she was found to be a Woman. Whereupon the Maid runs out, and calls up her Parents, who soon found out that they had married her not to a *Man*, but a *Woman*: Whereupon they carried the supposed Man, the next Day, to the General of the *Janizaries*, who, in the Absence of the *Grand Seignor*, was Governor of the City. When she was brought before him, he chid her soundly for her beastly Love; what, says he, are you not asham'd, an old Bedlam as you are, to attempt so notorious a Bestiality, and so filthy a Fact?

Away, Sir, says she! You do not know the Force of Love, and God grant you never may. At this absurd Reply, the Governor could scarce forbear Laughter, but commanded her, presently, to be back'd away and drown'd in the Deep; such was the unfortunate Issue of her wild Amours." See *Busbequin's* Travels into *Turkey*, P. 146, 147.

THE PETIT MAITRE. A Poem.
By a Lady.

I.

Tell me, gentle hob'dehoy!
Art thou Girl, or art thou Boy?
Art thou Man, or art thou Ape;
For thy Gesture and thy Shape;
And thy Features and thy Dress,
Such contraries do express:
I stand amaz'd, and at a Loss to know,
To what new Species thou thy Form dost owe;

II.

By thy Hair comb'd up behind,
Thou should'st be of *Womankind:*
But that damn'd forbidding Face,
Does the charming Sex disgrace;
Man, or Woman, thou are neither;
But a blot, a shame to either:
Nor dare to *Brutehood,* even to make Pretence;
For *Brutes* themselves, shew greater Signs of Sense.

III.

By thy *Jaws* all lank and thin;
By that forc'd unmeaning grin:
Thou appear'st to human Eyes,
Like some Ape of monstrous Size;
Yet an Ape thou can'st not be,
Apes are more Adroit than thee;
Thy Oddities so much my Mind perplex;
I neither can define thy Kind or Sex.

IV.

Art thou Substance, art thou Shade?
That thus monst'rously array'd,
Walking forth in open Day,
Dost our Senses quite dismay?
Unghastly yet, thou only can'st provoke,
Our Rage, our Detestation, and our Joke.

V.

If thou art a Man, forbear
Thus, this *motly* Garb to wear;
Do not Reason thus displace,
Do not Man-hood thus disgrace;
But thy Sex by Dress impart,
And appear like what thou art:
Like what thou art, said I, pray pardon me:
I mean, appear like what thou ought to be.

FINIS